VITTORIO SERRA

NEW PRACTICAL GUIDE OF
MILAN

★ *115 colour illustrations*
★ *detailed map of the town*

BONECHI EDIZIONI -IL TURISMO- - FIRENZE

© Copyright 1991 by Bonechi Edizioni "Il Turismo" S.r.l.
© Copyright 1996 by Bonechi Edizioni "Il Turismo" S.r.l.
© Copyright 1998 by Bonechi Edizioni "Il Turismo" S.r.l.
Via dei Rustici, 5 - 50122 FLORENCE
Tel. +39 (55) 239.82.24/25 - Fax +39 (55) 21.63.66
E-mail address: barbara@bonechi.com / bbonechi@dada.it
http://www.bonechi.com
Translation: Diana Vignali Clayton
Text revised by: Rosalynd Pio
Printing: BO.BA.DO.MA., Florence

ISBN 88-7204-199-6

HISTORICAL OUTLINE

Milan was founded by the Insubrian Celts around 400 b.C. After constant wars with the Gauls, the Romans succeeded in conquering it and thenceforth it became known as "Mediolanum" which means "in the middle of the plain". Its inhabitants rebelled against the Romans, having made an alliance with Hannibal, but in 196 b.C. the city was compelled to pay allegiance to the Romans and from that time onward it became the main industrial and commercial centre of northern Italy. In thus benefitted from the laws issued by the capital of the Empire and became very prosperous. Between the end of the Ist Cent. and the beginning of the IInd, Milan became Christian and a century later saw the founding of the Diocese with its first bishops who had an increasingly important role in the life of the city, especially at the time of St. Ambrose. It was the temporary seat of the Emperors and maintained its pre-eminence until the time of Theodosius, but with the advent of Honorius in 404, the privilege passed to Ravenna. In the period of the Barbarian invasions it fell prey to the Burgundians and in 539 suffered the wrath of Witigis.

During the Lombard domination between 568 and 774 Milan lost much of its former importance and was considered second to Pavia which the Lombards preferred. Even with the arrival of the Franks things did not change much; however, the activities of its bishops helped the recovery to a certain extent. Towards the middle of the tenth century, the clergy and the wealthy classes had gained political supremacy and succeeded in putting the city in order, and in making her commerce flourish once again.

The religious conflicts and the political and social contrasts between 1018 and 1045 caused the Milanese to side either with one or the other Emperor from the other side of the Alps in order to gain supremacy in Italy, until the age of the free cities. During the second half of the eleventh century and the first half of the following century, Milan was involved in the tremendous struggle between the Empire and the Papacy and this situation continued until the founding of the code of the free cities, a code which was developed very rapidly and enabled the city to face the terrible consequences of the Emperor Frederick, who destroyed the city in 1162. Within a few years the Lombard League was formed, reversing the situation by gaining a significant victory over the Emperor at Legnano.

Thus there followed a period in which the city settled down, despite desperate factional strife, until in the second half of the XIIIth Cent. there came the first signs of the seigniory. Powerful families struggled for supremacy within the city; eventually the Visconti family gained the upper hand and continued to rule despotically from 1330 to 1447. However they had the merit of producing a period of economic, artistic and cultural prosperity. With the end of the domination of the Viscontis came the short-lived Ambrosian Republic after which the seigniory of the Sforza family ruled over Milan between 1450 and 1535.

From this time onward the history of Milan became the history of the political activities of the Sforza family and was subject to all their ups and downs. They took part in the political events of Europe thanks to the activities of Ludovick the Moor. Charles VIII of France and other powerful rulers who were continually tempted by the Italian peninsula. In 1535 the struggle between Francis I of France and Charles V of Spain was resolved in favour of the latter and from 1535 until 1706 Milan was reluctantly subjected to the Spanish domination.

From 1706, following the Wars of Succession and the agreements reached by the contracting parties, Milan fell under the Austrian domination which

Museum of the Risorgimento. - Victor Emanuel IInd and Napoleon entering Milan.

lasted, apart from a brief interlude, until the Napoleonic regime, with the setting up of the Cisalpine Republic in 1797. However, under the Austrian rule, the industrial and cultural enterprise for which Milan was to become famous reburgened. During the Napoleonic supremacy the city became the capital, first of the Italian Republic and then of the Kingdom of Italy in 1805, but the rapid decline of Napoleon's fortunes enabled Austria to re-take Lombardy (1845) and to dominate it until 1859.

Although the Milanese were oppressed by the power of Austria, they were vehemently patriotic, and became an example to all the Italian people for the courage they showed in confronting the Austrian army during the epic "Five Days" (18th/23rd March 1848). Although their insurrection was put down due to the overwhelming numbers of their adversary, and it could not be turned to immediate use by the courageous promoters of Italian independence, it succeeded in making the Italian people wish to achieve the unification of Italy.

The history of Milan, as an independant political entity, ends in 1859 when the city took its place in the national community with all the weight of its political, religious and cultural history, its commercial and industrial enterprise behind it, constituting a vital and important part of the new state.

4

The area around Piazza del Duomo

Piazza del Duomo seen from above.

PIAZZA DEL DUOMO

This magnificent square is said to be the mirror of Milan and the Milanese. In fact all its citizens pour into it at every hour of the day; whether it is ablaze with sunlight or full of snow; they pass in a hurry and it almost seems that they pay no attention to its beauty, its gleaming space, its imposing, white cathedral. This is not true however, since the speed at which a Milanese thinks is the same as his rhythm of work and when he passes by he only needs a glance to comfort and excite him, to fill his heart with pride before disappearing into the underground or being swallowed up by the traffic.

The vast square, which is rectangular in shape, was given its present form in 1865 by the architect Giuseppe Mengoni. In the centre stands the **Monument to Victor Emanuel II** which is by Ercole Rosa (1896). This equestrian statue in bronze represents the King at the battle of San Martino, whilst the base shows the *entry of the Piedmontese and French troops into Milan* after the battle of Magenta (1859). The grandiose mass of the cathedral forms a background to the square and it is flanked on the left by the Palazzo Settentrionale (the Northern Palace) whose porticos open into the Victor Emmanuel arcade (Galleria Vittorio Emmanuele) and to the right by the *Palazzo Meridionale* (the Southern Palace) also with porticos, after which there are two buildings with loggias; at the other end the square is completed by the *Palazzo dell'orologio* (the Clock Palace).

THE CATHEDRAL OR DUOMO

The cathedral is the largest monument in Milan and the most gigantic and complex Gothic building in Italy. The colossal undertaking was started in 1386 and required centuries of work and the contribution of many generations. It was begun at the wish of the Milanese people urged by their archbishop, Antonio da Saluzzo and under the patronage of the Duke Gian Galeazzo Visconti. The pre-existing IXth Cent. church of Santa Maria Maggiore (St. Mary the Greater) was used to build the foundations on. The first architect is unknown but he was certainly inspired by Gothic cathedrals on the other side of the Alps. Some students of the cathedral attribute the original plan to a group of architects, amongst whom there was Simone da Orsenigo, who was the first engineer to construct it, Marco Frisone da Campione, Giovannino de Grassi and others. Through the centuries, however, various Italian, French and German artists participated in the design and construction and this is the reason for the enormous variety of nonetheless harmoniously blending styles in the building. In 1389 the Parisian, Nicolao De Bonaventuris took part in the work, and we owe the design of the great apse windows to him. Following this Giovannino and Salomone de Grassi directed the work as did also Gabriele Stornaloco from Piacenza, the Germans Johann of Freiburg, Heinrich of Gmülden, Ulrich of Fussyngen, the Fleming Corrado Bruges and Jean Mignot of Paris, after whom foreigners no longer participated in the project. In 1400, Filippino degli Organi was appointed master of the works and designed the fretwork of the apse, that of the vaults, of the terraces and of the capitals. From then onwards work on the colossal enterprise went ahead quickly, so much so that in 1418 Pope Martin V who was passing through Milan, was able to consecrate the high altar. In the second half of the XVth Cent., by decree of the Duke Francesco Sforza, the overseeing of the work was given to the Solaris and to the great Giovanni Antonio Amadeo who designed the drum. After the death of Amadeo (1522) work came to a temporary standstill, until the archbishop Carlo Borromeo in 1567 ordered the work to be continued under the direction of Pellegrini who designed the façade in classical Baroque style. In 1572 the archbishop Borromeo consecrated the cathedral once again. After

Duomo. - The façade.

Pellegrini, Martino Bassi and Lelio Buzzi and then in the XVIIth Cent., Francesco Maria Richini, first and then Carlo Buzzi who began the construction of the façade designed by Pellegrini, making some alterations to give it more of a Gothic look. In 1765, the tallest spire was raised. The gilded statue of the "Madonnina" (little Madonna) was hoisted into position in 1774. In 1805, Napoleon entrusted Carlo Amati with the task of finishing the work on the façade. The construction of the spires and the staircase turrets around the drum continued throughout the XIXth Cent. The doors

Duomo. - The south side.

in the façade, except for the central Pogliaghi door (1908) were variously placed in position from 1948 to 1965.

DIMENSIONS AND CHARACTERISTICS OF THE BUILDING. - As regards the surface covered, the Duomo of Milan (11,700 sqms) is the second largest church in Italy and the third largest in the world, surpassed only by St. Peter's in Rome and by the Cathedral of Seville in Spain. The external length is 157 metres; the width of the nave and aisles: 66 metres; the transept is 92 metres wide. The façade is 56 metres high and 67.90 metres wide. There are 135 spires and the tallest with the gold "Madonnina" is 108.50 metres

Duomo. - The "Madonnina" at the top of the highest spire.

high. The facings are of Candoglia marble, pinky white with bluish veining. There are 2,245 statues outside the cathedral; if one includes the internal ones, the figure comes to 3,159 (excluding those in the embrasures of the windows). There are 96 gigantic gargoyles.

THE FAÇADE. - The lower part, up to the first series of windows is Baroque and was executed in the XVIth Cent. upon designs by Pellegrini. The upper part, executed in the following centuries, was remodelled in the Gothic style. Six very high pillars surmounted by spires divide the five great XVIth Cent. doors from each other and two rows of windows crowned by balconies which as they go upwards join together towards the centre to

Duomo. - The richly carved giant pilasters on the façade.

form the cusp. The bases on which the pillars rest are decorated with reliefs representing stories from the Bible, which were carved in the XVIIth and XVIIIth Cents., whilst the bases of the pillars themselves are decorated with *Telamons* of the same epoch. The higher statues, on shelves, represent *Apostles* and *Prophets* and were sculpted at the beginning of the XIXth Cent. The freizes of the first doorway are also by Crespi, while the bronze door with panels representing *Episodes in the Life of St. Ambrose* is by Giannino Castiglioni (1950); the magnificent doorway of the central entrance, decorated with rich parastas of flowers and animals, was based upon designs by Francesco M. Richini; while the beautiful door in bronze with decorations representing *Episodes from the Life of Mary* is by Ludovico Pogliaghi (1984-1908); the freize of the fourth doorway is by Crespi

Duomo. - The apse.

and the bronze door with panels representing the *History of Milan from the destruction by Barbarossa to the Victory of Legnano* is by Franco Lombardi but was finished by Virgilio Pessina (1950): the freize of the fifth doorway is by Carlo Biffi, whilst the door in bronze representing the *Salient Episodes in the History of the Cathedral*, is by Luciano Menguzzi (1965).

INTERIOR. - The overwhelming proportions of the cathedral and the mystical evocativeness of the soft light that filters through the multi-coloured stained - glass windows draw one's thoughts up to the Creator of all things. The cathedral has 52 very high polystyle pillars which support the vault, and is divided into 5 aisles. Foliate decoration adorns the pillar capitals whilst the central nave pillars are surrounded by a garland of

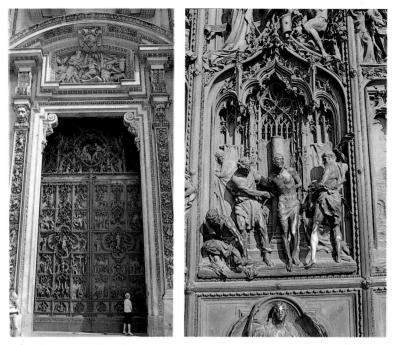

Duomo. - Left: **the central door.** Right: **one of the panels on the central door.** Further right: **view up one of the aisles.**

niches containing statues of Saints. Around the deep apse runs an ample ambulatory. The floor which has recently been renovated, was based on a design by Pellegrini. The central nave which leads to the drum and the central nave of the transept are twice as wide as the side aisles. The great central doorway of the internal façade is by Fabio Mangone and is surmounted by statues of *St. Ambrose and St. Charles* by Pompeo Marchesi and Gaetano Monti respectively.

THE RIGHT AISLE. - 1st span, *Tomb of the archbishop Ariberto da Intimiano*, inventor of the XIth Cent. Carroccio. Above the tomb there is a XIth Cent. Lombard copper *Crucifix* of great interest — a reproduction (the original being in the Duomo Museum). To the left, a plaque with an inscription commemorating the year of the foundation of the cathedral (1386). — 2nd span, the *Mausoleum of the archbishop Ottone Visconti* (died 1295) in red marble, (XVth Cent.). 4th span, the *Sarcophagus of Marco Carelli* by Filippino degli Organi (1406). — 5th span, plaque with the plan for the façade of the cathedral presented by G. Brentano in 1886; on the left, *Monument to Cardinal Vimercati* by Bambaia. The 26 panes of the large windows, with *Stories from the New Testament* are only a part of a great window which was reconstructed by Bertini. — 6th span, altar by Pellegrini with an altarpiece representing the *Visit of St. Peter to St. Agatha* by F. Zuccari (1597) — 7th span, altar by Pellegrini. — 8th span, altar by Pellegrini with a marble altarpiece with a *Sacred Conversation* of 1396. The transept from the centre of which rises the soaring drum begins here.

12

Duomo. - Some staggeringly beautiful stained-glass windows.

THE RIGHT TRANSEPT. - On the far right side of the right transept, monument to Gian Giacomo Medici, known as the "Medeghino" (d. 1555) marquis of Marignano, and a general of Charles V; a masterpiece by Leone Leoni (1560-63). The monument is decorated with bas-reliefs and a bronze statue of the dead general in Roman armour in the central shrine. The statue to the left represents *Militia* and the bas-relief dominating it, the *Adda*; to the right, the statue of *Peace* and above, the bas-relief representing the *Ticino*. The statues on the external columns represent *Prudence* and *Fame*. On the walls at the end of the nave we find a small altar in precious marble of the XVIth Cent., decorated with 2 statues in copper donated by Pope Pius IV (the large window with *Stories of St. James the Elder* is by Corrado de Mochis 1554-1564).

In the central aisle apse of the transept, there is the Chapel of St. Giòvanni Bono, Bishop of Milan (XVIth Cent.); the three windows show *Episodes from the life of the Saint*, by Giovanni Bertini.

In the left aisle of the right arm of the transept, between two little doors, we find the underground passage to the Archbishop's Palace, dominated by a stupendous stained glass window representing *Scenes from the Life of*

Duomo. - The monument to Gian Giacomo de' Medici of Marignano, by Leone Leoni.

Saint Catherine of Alexandria by Biagio and Giuseppe Archimboldi (1556). The next altar, has a marble altar piece with the *Presentation of Mary at the Temple* by Bambaia (1543). In the stained glass window, *Story of St. Martin* — further ahead, on a pedestal, a statue of *St. Bartholomew flayed alive* by Marco d'Agreste (1562), which is very famous but of little artistic value. On the following altar a marble altar piece with the *Martyrdom of St. Agnes* by C. Beretta and a statue of *St. Ambrose.*

THE DRUM. - To get to the presbytery one crosses the magnificent drum (68 metres high), which is octagonal in shape and rises above four very high pointed arches. On the pinnacles of the arches there are busts of the *Doctors of the Church* by Cristoforo Solari; the statues placed on lintels along the ring of internal arches (60 in all) are of the XVth Cent. On the floor at the joining of the arms of the cross there is a bronze barrier which encloses the "Scurolo" or Vault of St. Charles beneath.

THE PRESBYTERY. - Ten pillars linked to each other by a marble enclosure, surround the presbytery which Pellegrini raised to make space for the crypt. With their backs to the pillars at the entrance, stand two pulpits in

Duomo. - Left: **view up one of the side-aisles.** Right: **the flayed St. Bartholomew, by Marco d'Agrate (1562).**

embossed bronze and copper representing the *Symbols of the Evangelists* (left), and the *Doctors of the Church* (right); on both parapets *Stories from the Old and New Testaments* (XVIth-XVIIth Cents.). In the first part of the presbytery, which is occupied by the senatorial *Choir*, also two colossal organs, one on either side, of the XVIth Cent. Further ahead, is the staircase leading to the Sanctuary containing the Great Altar; beautiful rich decoration covers the original altar consecrated by Martin V in 1418. Above stands the great ciborium in gilded bronze flanked by two *Angels* as candleholders supported by eight little columns, beautifully shaped by Andrea Pellizzone (1581-90), designed by Pellegrini. It encloses the Tabernacle, supported by four *Angels* and decorated with reliefs representing *Episodes from the Life of Jesus* and crowned by small statues of *Christ* and the *Apostles* by the Solaris (1561). The whole sanctuary is surrounded by a magnificent 3 level choir stall in walnut carved between 1572 and 1620 upon a design by Pellegrini. In the vault towards the altar there is a copper grate with *God the Father* by Jacopino da Tradate and under it lies the *Holy Nail* which, tradition has, was given to Constantine by Helen and then found by St. Ambrose at a blacksmith's.

CRYPT. - Two doors in the façade of the sacresty behind the choir-stalls lead to the crypt. The whole thing is by Pellegrini, whilst the stucco which

Duomo. - The Vault (Scurolo) of St. Charles.

decorates the vaults was added in the XVIth Cent. From here going down a few steps, one reaches the underground chapel called the *Scurolo di San Carlo* (Vault of St. Charles). Octagonal in shape, it was built upon the designs of Richini (1606). It is richly decorated in silver leaf with eight reliefs on the ceiling representing the deeds of the Saint, executed by artists of the XVIIth Cent. The body of St. Charles, in papal vestments decorated with gems, is enclosed in a rich urn of rock crystal.

THE AMBULATORY. - The Ambulatory surrounds the presbytery from which it is separated by a lovely marble enclosure by Pellegrini. Along the upper part runs an attic with panels, divided by statues, with bas-reliefs representing *Stories from the Life of Mary* of the XVIIth Cent. Following the external side; the first span: a great canvas with a reproduction of the XIVth Cent. *Annunciation* from the Santissima Annunziata in Florence, copied by Bronzino in 1580 and given to St. Charles by Francesco Ist of the Medicis. Next comes the portal of the southern sacresty stupendously ornate and by the German Hans von Fernach assisted by Porrino and Giovannino De Grassi. Inside the sacresty, above the entrance we find the *Martyrdom of St. Thecla* by Aurelio Luini (1592). The basin to the right with a medallion in the cusp with *Jesus and the Samaritan* Woman, is by Giovannino De Grassi (1396). To the left in the niche, *Christ at the Column* by Cristoforo Solari. The big XVIIth Cent. walnut cupboards, which cover the lower part of the walls, contain the precious objects which form part of the Treasure, amongst which the famous painted processional cusped panel with the *Madonna of the Idea* bearing the forged signature of Michelino da Besozzo. Beyond the sacristy door in the second span are the remains of an antique frescoes of the XVth Cent. with the *Madonna suckling the Child* known as the *Virgin of Help*; above this, on a large gothic corbel, the beautiful statue of *Martin V[th]*, by Jacopino da Tradate (1424). The plaque below covers the remains of the condottieri Nicolò and Francesco Piccinino. Next comes the *Monument to Cardinal Marino Caracciolo* (d. 1538) executed by Bambaia. Third span, framed marble slab known as "*Chrismon Sancti Ambrosii*", and bas-relief of 1389 by a German artist, of *Deposition* and two *Angels*. Fourth span, memorial of the consecration of the church, by the archbishop Carlo Borromeo 20th September 1572. The three stained glass windows of the apse contain *Stories from the New Testament*, *Stories from the Apocalypse*, and *Stories from the Old Testament*. Flanking the great windows we find statues of the XIV-XVth Cents. Fifth span, under glass, IIIrd Cent. *Crucifix* dressed in liturgical vestments. Sixth span: *Statue of Pius IV Blessing* by Angelo Marini (1567). The frescoes representing the *Crucifix between the Virgin and Saints* and the *Madonna with Child and St. John the Baptist* were both done at the beginning of the XVth Cent. Seventh span: the marvellous *Portal* of the northern sacresty, by Giacomo da Campione (XIVth Cent.); the cusp above the portal contains a relief of the *Redemeer Blessing*. Inside, the vault frescoed with *Angels* by Camillo Procaccini (1611), whilst the floor is by Marco da Corona (beginning of the XVth Cent.) in the niche we find the statue, of particular interest, of the *Redeemer* by Antonio da Viggiù.

THE LEFT TRANSEPT. - Along the right aisle we find two altars and upon them two marble altar pieces with *St. Thecla among the Lions* by Carlo Beretta (1754) and the *Crucifix and Saints* by Marcantonio Prestinari (1605). The beautiful stained glass window shows the stories of *St. John of Damascus* by Nicolò da Varallo (XVth Cent.). The small door in the wall beyond leads to the "Stair of the Princes" which leads to the terraces; in the past it was reserved for important people only. In the small apse of the middle nave, one finds the chapel of the *Madonna of the Tree*, designed by Richini in Baroque style; on the altar *Madonna and Child* by Elia Vincenzo Buzzi (1768). In the central aisle itself, in front of the altar, the celebrated bronze *Trivulzio Candlestick* with seven arms, 5 metres high, by a French XIIIth Cent. artist. The famous candlestick was given by a Trivulzio in 1562. In the left aisle, the altar with statues of the XVth and XVIth Cents. including *St. Jerome* and *St. Augustine* by Cristofaro Solari.

THE LEFT AISLE. - The eighth span: altar by Pellegrini, with a canvas by Barocci (1603). The seventh span: above the altar is the *Espousal of the Virgin* by Enea Salmeggia (1600). The sixth span: above the altar a wooden *Crucifix* which was carried by St. Charles in procession during the plague of 1576. The fifth span: *Monument to Alessio Tarchetta*, captain at the time of Francesco Sforza, completely remade in 1832; fragments of the original by Amadeo are to be found in the Museum of the Castello Sforzesco. The fourth span: window designed by Pellegrini with *Stories of the four Crowned Saints* and executed by Corrado de Mochis (1568). The third span: *Monument of the three Archimboldi archibishops*, attributed to Alessi. The second span: two red marble slabs from Verona with reliefs representing eight of the *Apostles* from the end of the XIIth Cent. To the left, between the columns, the Baptistery in the form of a shrine, designed by Pellegrini; the font is an ancient Roman porphyry urn.

Duomo. - The Trivulzio candlestick, by a French artist.

CLIMB TO THE TERRACES. - Once one has visited the cathedral both inside and outside and seen the view of the right side and the façade together from the Piazzetta Reale (royal square), a visit to the terraces is indispensable. One gets to the terraces through the two entrances at the far end of the sides of the cathedral where there is a climb up 158 steps. A lift is provided, however, at the corner of the transepts towards the apse on the outside of the cathedral. The feeling experienced by the visitor is unforgettable, unique, entirely different from the sensations given by Giotto's Campanile in Florence, or the dome of St. Peter's in the Vatican, or even the tower of the Town Hall in Siena from all of which one can enjoy stupendous views of the respective cities and the surrounding hills.

**Duomo. - Up on the terraces, visitors experience the unforgetta-
ble sight of the forest of spires and statues surrounding them.**

From the terraces of Milan cathedral one not only grasps the vast size and
beauty of this monument, but the mere contact with the great blocks of
marble, the forest of spires of every size, the numerous statues, the
gigantic gargoyles, is absolutely fascinating. The drum also arouses
admiration; it is Amedeo's masterpiece (1490) and is surmounted by the
tallest spire crowned with the famous statue of the Madonnina in gilded
bronze, which is 4.16 metres high and by G. Perego (1774).

The Royal Palace.

THE ROYAL PALACE

The building stands in the rectangular square on the southern side of the cathedral; its front is neoclassical and it has two side wings. Its origins are very old and during its history it has witnessed many changes. In the XIIth Cent., the **Broletto Vecchio**, which was where the Consuls, who governed the Free Commune, had their headquarters, was built on this site. In 1310, the Viscontis established themselves there, and in 1330 Azzone transformed the palace into a sumptuous residence, making it the Ducal court of the Viscontis. In 1385 the Viscontis went to live in the Castle when the front of the palace was demolished to make room for the cathedral. In the XVIth and XVIIth Cents. the building was radically restructured and became the seat of the Spanish governors; in addition, it was the site of the first Milanese opera house. In 1771-78, when the Milanese state was under Austrian domination, the archduke Ferdinand ordered the architect Giuseppe Piermarini to modify the building once more, destroying the façade and rearranging the great rooms, according to the needs of the times. With the Unification of Italy, it became the Royal Palace and later it became a Museum containing a large collection of artefacts produced during the Milanese neoclassical period.

Duomo Museum. - One of the rooms with sketches, casts, models and sculpture.

THE DUOMO MUSEUM

The Museum occupies a number of ground floor rooms of the Royal Palace and provides a fascinating overall view of how the cathedral developed through the centuries. The statues and decorative elements, which succeed each other in the chronologically arranged rooms, and of which the originals have been placed inside the Museum, prove how the Duomo was a stimulating focus for artistic endeavour throughout Lombard history.

Room 1 - Great Copper-gilt embossed effigy of the *Heavenly Father* by Beltramino da Rho (1416).

Room 2 (or of the Origins). - In the centre: Statue of *Gian Galeazzo Visconti as St. George* by Giorgio Solari (1404). On the walls, three marble statues (*Two Angels* and a *Prophet*) once on the Carelli spire - Bourgogne School end of the XIVth Cent. *Head of the Redeemer* and *St. Agnes* by Briosco. *Madonna and Child*: painted wooden statue by Bernardo da Venezia.

Room 3 (or Visconti Room) - Once the stables of the Royal Palace. The ground plan is rectangular and contains several Visconti-era objects by Rhineland/Bohemian and Lombard craftsmen. To wit, *St. Peter the Apostle, St. John the Evangelist* and the plaster cast of the *Monument to Pope Martin V[th]* made for the Duomo by Jacopino da Tradate (1421) as well as various *Prophets* and *Saints*.

Room 4 (or of the Music Chapel). - XVth Cent. Polyphonic music scores.

Duomo Museum. - Head of the Redeemer.

ROOM 5 (or Room of the Drum). - Contains a graphic documentation on the building of the drum and on the works it includes: a remarkable *St. Peter the Apostle*, attributed to Jacobello dalle Masegne (XIVth Cent).

ROOM 6 (or of the Sforza era). - In the centre a statue of *Galeazzo Maria Sforza* inside a Terracotta apse - a unique example of Lombard sculpture, flanked by *Shieldbearing Warriors* of the Mantegazza School together with an *Angel bearing a Crown of Thorns*. Various *Sforza shields* on the walls.

ROOM 7 (or the Embossed Brass Room). - Remarkable *Crucifix* by Ariberto (1040) in embossed copper and brass; XIVth Cent. Rhineland School: *Madonna and Child with two Angels*; and a great *Easter Candlestick* (XVth Cent. Lombard School).

ROOM 8 (or Sforza Room). - Pavia and Milanese School sculpture: a remarkable *St. Paul the Hermit* (1470); *St. Lucy* and *St. Agnes*, attributed to Briosco (1491). Also: Flemish Tapestry with *Deposition*.

ROOM 9 (or of the Amadeo Spire). - Photographic documentation of the "torrino" or spire built by Giovanni Antonio Amadeo (1517); the two XVIth Cent. statues of *Virtue* and *St. Barbara* and a XVth Cent. Flemish altar - front arras with *Scenes of the Passion*.

ROOM 10 (or of the Borromeos). - Artefacts revealing the Counter-Reform influence of Carlo and Federico Borromeo (*Altar-front arras of St. Charles Borromeo*) and the *Miracle of the Woman in Labour* by Cerano (1610); embossed silver candlestick (1610) and two choir-stalls.

ROOM 11 (or Tapestry Room). - On the walls: Four tapestry hangings from the series given by the Duke of Mantua to St. Carlo Borromeo, showing *Moses receiving the Tablets of the Law*; the *Crossing of the Red Sea*; *Moses and the Bronze Serpent*; and *Putti playing*. Moreover, *Jesus with the Doctors*

Duomo Museum. - St. George, by Giorgio Solari (1404).

in the Temple, an early work by Tintoretto and a wooden *Crucifix* of the XVIIth Cent. Venetian School.

ROOM 12 (or of the Models). - Various sculptures from the 1500s to the 1700s: *St. Helena* and *Madonna in Exstasy among Angels* by Marini (1565); *Sacrifice of Elija* and *Abraham about to sacrifice Isaac* by Vismara (XVIIth Cent.); *St. Agapitus* and *St. Ambrose* by M. Prestinari (1610) and the *Flight into Egypt* (1624) one of the paintings by Biffi, in this room. Wooden and terracotta models for Mannerist and Baroque statues.

ROOM 13 (or of the "Madonnina"). - Terracotta models of the famous "Madonnina" placed on the tallest spire of the Duomo in 1774 and detail of the *Head* in wood (1771) by Giuseppe Perego, who also modelled the *Warrior Saint* and a terracotta model of *Hercules slaying the Lion of Nemea,* as well as terracotta models by various artists.

ROOM 14 (or of the XIXth Cent.). - Various examples of restauration and work on the façade, spires and windows. A remarkable *Prophet Beseleel* by Martegani (1867) and *St. Catherine of Alexandria* by Buzzi.

ROOM 15 (Gallery of the Graphs). - A step-by-step illustration of how the Duomo was built from the beginning to the present day, including the five projects presented through the centuries for the façade.

ROOM 16 (or of the Great Model). - In the middle of the room: a great *wooden model of the Duomo*, begun around 1520 with the winning façade presented at the world-wide competition of 1886 by the architect Giuseppe Brentano, in 1888. Opposite: the other *wooden project* for the façade presented by Luca Beltrami, carved by Gaetano Moretti also in 1888. Left: *wooden model for the façade* in Gothic-Baroque style, by Castelli, dated 1656. Right: another project presented by Galliori in 1786. Also a *model of the old bell-tower.*

ROOM 17 (or of the Bronze Doors). - Sculpture for the five portals of the façade. Of particular interest: *The Sermon on the Mount* (fifteen gilded bronze models) by Francesco Messina (1977).

ROOM 18 and 19 (or the Conservation and Restoration Room). - Interesting documentation concerning the restoration work carried out for the survival of the ancient structures, using modern technology and facilities.

ROOM 20 (or Vestments Room). - Access to this room is through Room 12 and its contents are not arranged in the chronological order that has been kept-to in the rest of the Museum. It contains an important collection of ecclesiastical vestments and liturgical objects from the Cathedral Chapter Sacristy. A remarkable *gold and silver woven Chasuble* (1805) used during the Coronation of Napoleon, as well as various copes and altar-frontals.

SAN GOTTARDO IN CORTE

The construction of the church which is incorporated in the Royal Palace, (the entrance is from via Pecorari) goes back to the first half of the XIVth Cent. Azzone Visconti had it built as a chapel for the ducal court, and tradition has it that the Cremonese architect Francesco Pecorari was in charge of the project.
The Gothic character of the outside remains: the portal, the apse with its cusped windows, the loggia higher up and the elegant belltower by Pecorari. The bottom part of the belltower is square then it becomes octogonal with little stone columns at the corners; it has a single opening on each of the lower levels, two openings at the fourth level, while two layers of columned arches adorn the fifth level, above which there is a delightful gallery of columns surmounted by a conic cusp with a statue of the Angel Gabriel in copper on the top.

THE INTERIOR. - The interior was completely transformed in the neoclassical period, and contains a fragment of a fresco of the *Crucifixion*, which used to be outside, painted towards the middle of the XIVth Cent. by a follower of Giotto; also a canvas by Cerano of *St. Charles in Glory* and the *Sepulchre of Azzone Visconti* by Giovanni di Balduccio.

San Gottardo in Corte. - The belltower.

Victor Emanuel Arcade. - The interior from the central octagon.

THE VICTOR EMANUEL ARCADE

Galleria Vittorio Emanuele II links the Cathedral square to the Scala square. Building began in 1865 under Giuseppe Mengoni who died, after falling from the scaffolding, when it was almost completed in 1877. The arcade is known as the "drawing-room" of Milan because it is lined with luxurious cafés, elegant shops and important bookshops. It is cross shaped, one arm 196 metres long and the other 105 metres. The cupola is made of iron and glass and at its highest point is 47 metres high. The four mosaics in the lunettes above the octagon show Europe, Africa, Asia and America and in the lunettes at the end of each arm: Agriculture, Art, Science, and Industry.

Piazza della Scala. - The theatre of La Scala.

PIAZZA DELLA SCALA

In the centre we find the *Monument to Leonardo da Vinci* by Pietro Magni (1872). Four statues of the Milanese disciples of Leonardo, *Marco d'Oggiono, G. Antonio Boltraffio, Andrea Salaino and Cesare da Sesto* stand at the corners of the pedestal. The square looks onto the La Scala Theatre and to the right **Palazzo Marini**, seat of the town council from 1860. This magnificent building which is still one of the most beautiful in Milan, was begun in 1553 by Galeazzo Alessi, and commissioned by Tomaso Marini, a Genoese, but he was unable to finish it before his death. The town council then decided to finish it and appointed Luca Beltrami (1886-92) who finished the façade on the La Scala square and constructed the great internal staircase which leads to the floors above. The original façade looks onto Piazza S. Fedele. Inside, besides the beautiful portico courtyard with twin columns and loggia, richly decorated with statues and reliefs, there is also the interesting **Sala dell'Alessi** decorated with stucco and paintings by Ottavio Semini.

LA SCALA THEATRE

La Scala is the most famous opera house in the world both because of the high level of its performances, and also because it is the testing ground of all the world's singers and musicians. It represents the final goal and highest aspiration of every opera singer. It was built in 1778 by Maria Giuseppe Piermarini, where the church of S. Maria dalla Scala used to stand (it was founded in 1381 by Beatrice Regina della Scala the wife of Bernabò Visconti). The outside is rather simple with a neoclassical façade and is preceeded by a small porticoed atrium with a bas-relief of *Apollo's chariot* (1778) in the tympanum.

THE INTERIOR. - The entrance hall there are statues of *Rossini, Bellini, Verdi* and *Donizetti* and a bust of *Stendhal*. The hall itself is horseshoe-shaped with four tiers of boxes and two galleries, and is decorated sumptuously in neoclassical style, faithfully reconstructed after the serious damage suffered during the 1943 bombings. The theatre holds 2800 spectators.

In the palace with porticos to the left of La Scala, we find the **Theatre Museum** (entrance at no. 2). It contains a precious collection of objects and relics relating to the history of La Scala Theatre and to theatrical art from classical antiquity to modern times. The Verdi collection, in two rooms, with a well-documented collection of pictures and drawings relating to Verdi, and autographed scores of his compositions, is particularly interesting. The theatre library includes the private collection of Renato Simoni and Ruggero Ruggeri. Altogether, it is one of the largest and most complete theatrical collections, with around 80,000 volumes, on Italian and foreign productions, drama, criticism and the history of the theatre.

Theatre Museum of La Scala. - Portraits of Giacomo Puccini and Giuseppe Verdi. Right: **the famous horse-shoe-shaped interior of the theatre.**

SAN FEDELE

Looks onto piazza San Fedele, where the *monument to Alessandro Manzoni* by Francesco Barzagli stands (1883). The building of the church was begun in 1569 by Pellegrini for St. Charles Borromeo. It was then continued by Martino Bassi and Richini and eventually finished in the XIX century. The façade is typically XVIth Cent. in its decoration and architecture. It was badly damaged during the bombings in the last war and was later restored. The relief of the *Assumption* in the tympanum is by Monti.

THE INTERIOR has a single nave, divided into two spans supported by columns against the walls; there are several good paintings including: on the first altar to the right: *Saint Ignatius gloriosus* by Cerano; the second altar has curiously grouped columns supported by angels and *Four Saints* by Bernardino Campi; the first altar to the left, *Deposition* by Simone Peterzano. The XVIth Cent. engraved confessionals which are very beautiful, are the work of the Taurinis, while the wooden inlaid choir-stall near the apse, which comes from the demolished church of S. Maria della Scala, is attributed to Anselmo Del Conte (XVIth Cent.). The sacristy (entrance after the second altar to the right) is said to be the most beautiful in Milan with its stupendous carved cupboards.

Casa degli Omenoni. - The façade caryatids (Omenoni).

Behind the church of San Fedele runs the narrow via Omenoni, which gets its name from the XVIth Cent. house at no. 3, called **Casa degli Omenoni** (house of the big men) because of the eight gigantic caryatids that adorn the lower part of the façade. This beautiful house was built in the second half of the XVIth Cent. by the sculptor Leone Leoni, for his own use. The via Omenoni leads to the characteristic and secluded piazza Belgioioso with, to the right, the imposing neoclassical *Palazzo Belgioioso* constructed by Giuseppe Piermarini (1772-81) by order of Prince Alberico III Belgioioso. The building opposite is *Palazzo Besana*, built in 1815, while the brick house at the end, at the corner of via Morone, is the **House of Alessandro Manzoni**, where the writer lived from 1814 until his death on the 22nd May 1873. To-day it is the *National Centre of Studies on Manzoni* and the **Manzoni Museum**, which includes the poet's study with furniture and books, the bedroom where the poet died, and a collection of sketches, relics and books. Via Morone leads into via Alessandro Manzoni, where immediately to the right in an imposing building (no. 12) we find the entrance to the Poldi-Pezzoli Museum.

The Poldi-Pezzoli Museum from Via Alessandro Manzoni.

POLDI-PEZZOLI MUSEUM

The Museum contains the remarkable art collection that the aristocrat Gian Giacomo Poldi-Pezzoli, one of the most knowledgeable and enthusiastic art collectors of the last century, succeeded in assembling in his residence. The number and quality of the works of art in the collection bear witness to the discernment and whole-heartedness of this private collector. At his death (1879) he left the precious collection or art foundation to the city.

THE INTERIOR. - The ground floor beyond the entrance, where the *Portrait of Gian Giacomo Poldi-Pezzoli* by Francesco Hayez is displayed, houses the **Armoury** which has a collection of firearms, halberds, swords, daggers etc.; the **Fresco Room**, with the magnificent *Delft tapestry*, with knightly scenes (1602), the *Hood* from a Bishop's Cope with designs from Botticelli, *frontals of altars* of the XVth Cent. and marvellous *Venetian mirrors*; the **Archeological and Carpet room**, with fragments of coptic textiles, the Täbriz Carpet (around 1560) vases, bronzes, silver-ware, gold, and bronze and iron-age arms. Returning to the entrance, one climbs the picturesque staircase with the Baroque marble fountain by Petiti, at the bottom and the great *Landscapes* by Alessandro Magnasco, on the walls, also XVIIIth Cent. statues. On the first floor in the vestibule, *bust of Count Meipperg* by Canova and *bust of Rosa Poldi-Pezzoli* by Lorenzo Bartolini; among the paintings *Allegory* by Giulio Campi. From here one passes into the **rooms**

Poldi-Pezzoli Museum. - Portrait of a young woman, by Antonio del Pollaiolo.

of the Lombards which display the works of Lombard Masters of the Renaissance, amongst which the most important are: *Madonna with Child* a masterpiece by Vincenzo Foppa to whom is also attributed the *Portrait of Francesco Brivio*; *Madonna suckling the Child* and *Rest during the flight to Egypt* by Andrea Solario of whom there are two other works; *Madonna and Child who is picking a flower*, masterpiece by Giovanni Antonio Boltraffio; *the Mystic wedding of Saint Catherine* by Bernardino Luini of whom there are other works to admire; *Madonna and Saints* by Gaudenzio Ferrari and together with other paintings there are precious painted wooden sculptures of the XVIth Cent. showing the *Marriage of the Virgin*. Returning to the vestibule, one enters the **Room of the Foreigners** with *Landscape* and *Genre Scenes* by Jan Brueghel the Elder and four small tables by Lucas Cranach with the *Portrait of Martin Luther* and of *Kate von Bora, St. John the Baptist* and the *Immaculate Conception*. There follows the *Stucco room*, which is decorated in XVIIIth Cent. style with a small Saxony porcelain statue of *Augustus the Strong*, in the glass case there is a precious collection of porcelain from Saxony, Vienna, Capodimonte and Sèvres. In the **Golden Room**, the most famous and valuable works belonging to the Museum are kept. On the floor lies the famous Persian *carpet* with hunting scenes dating from 1523. Among the numerous paintings we mention *Madonna and Child* by Andrea Mantegna; *Lament over the Dead Christ* by Giovanni Bellini; *Madonna and Child* and *Lament over the Dead Christ* two paintings by Sandro Botticelli; *St. Nicholas of Tolentino* by Piero della Francesca; *Portrait of a young woman* a masterpiece by Antonio Pollaiolo; *Grey Lagoon* by Francesco Guardi. In addition we find works by Bartolomeo Montagna, Antonio Vivarini and a masterly bronze bust by Gian Lorenzo Bernini representing the *Bishop Ulpiano Volpi*. At the far end in the **Romanelli Room**, which takes its name from the *Tapestry* of Antwerp, based on a cartoon by G. Francesco Romanelli, we find besides paintings by Maratta, Bernardo Cavallino and others, a wooden Tuscan *Crucifix* of the XIVth Cent. Returning to the Golden Room, we find the entrance to the **Black Room** with a table in marble marquetry work from the Florentine Opificio delle Pietre Dure (Factory of the Semiprecious Stones) (XVIIth Cent.). In the corner, is the famous sculpture by Lorenzo Bartolini of *Faith in God*. Among the numerous paintings are the *Triptych* by Mariotto Albertinelli; *Faith* by Luca Signorelli; *St. Catherine of Alexandria* by Bergognone, *Portrait of Cardinal Carlo de' Medici*. In the following **Murano Glass Room**, there is an exceptional glass collection of the XVth to the XIXth Cent., displayed in two large glass cases. Amongst the paintings we note the *Annunciation* by Francesco Pesellino; *Madonna and Child with Saints* by Sodoma; various miniatures by artists from Florence, Umbria, and the Marche (XVth Cent.) and two Tyrolean painted wooden bas-reliefs (XVIth Cent.). Through the two doors one passes to the **Dante Room** decorated in neo-Gothic floral style of the late XIXth Cent. In the glass cases: Wedgewood and Oriental porcelain, silver etc. In the central glass case *Dante* by Giuseppe Bertini. Returning to the Black Room one passes into the **Tapestry Room** which takes its name from the tapestry with a scene of *Battle of Knights*. In this room there are various interesting paintings including: *St. Charles Borromeo receives the Oblates* by Alessandro Magnasco; *Portrait* by Giuseppe Ribera; *the Death of St. Jerome, Joshua stops the Sun* and *Strength and Wisdom* three works by G. Battista Tiepolo and other works by Bernardo Strozzi, Francesco Morazzone, Francesco Guardi, Palma il Vecchio, Luca Giordano. There follows the **Golden Cabinet** with a precious collection of jewels, diadems, diamonds and golden objects and figures, gold and silver caskets, etc. In the **Room of Ghislandi**, known also as Brother Galgario, we find one of his

Poldi-Pezzoli Museum. - Madonna and Child (detail from the polyptych), **by Cristoforo Moretti.**

masterpieces: *Gentleman with Tricorn hat.* The other works are by Francesco Zuccarelli, Domenico Feti, Rosalba Carriera, Francesco Guardi, Bernardo Bellotto and others. In the **Room of Perugino** by whom *Madonna with Angels* was painted, are other works by artists of the Veneto, Emilia, Tuscany and Umbria. *Madonna and Child, Angels and Saints* by Pietro Lorenzetti; *St. Maurelius* by Cosmè Tura; *Samson and Delilah* by Francesco Morone; *Crucifixion* by Giovanni Bellini; *Lament over the Dead Christ* by Filippo Lippi; *St. Jerome* by Antoniazzo Romano as well as works by Bartolomeo di Giovanni, Carlo Crivelli, Francesco Bonsignori. In the **Venetian Room** we find one of the best works of Cima da Conegliano with the *Triumph of Bacchus and Arianna* and also by him *Head of a Saint.* We also find other works by artists of the Venetian Renaissance including *The Holy Family with St. John* and *St. Catherine*, two works by Lorenzo Lotto; *the Annunciation* by Marco Palmezzano; the *Visit of the Doctor* by Bonifazio de' Pitati and others by the school of Carpaccio and Mantegna.

Piazza San Babila, church of St. Babilas and Lion Column.

Via Manzoni is one of the liveliest main thoroughfares of Milan, with XIXth Cent. houses on either side which have been made into comfortable hotels, banks, insurance companies and beautiful shops. At no. 11 we find *Palazzo Bigli* of the XVIth Cent. with ornate portals, pendentives and two medallions in relief of the *Annunciation*. After the entrance into via Monte Napoleone (on the right) we find the church of *S. Francesco da Paola* of the XVIIIth Cent. and the street continues until at the end we reach the **Arches of Porta Nuova** (New Gate) with two barrel-vaults of black and white marble once part of the city walls built to defend the town from Barbarossa in 1156. On the external façade there is a marble tabernacle with the *Madonna and Child between Saints Ambrose, Gervase and Protasius* in the manner of Giovanni di Balduccio, put there by Azzone Visconti in the XIVth Cent., whilst on the internal front are busts in niches, tablets and funeral plaques. Turning back we proceed along via Monte Napoleone which is the most aristocratic street of Milan with XIXth Cent. houses, some of which are neoclassical. It is lined on either side with luxury shops, especially antique shops. Many of the streets which lead to the XIXth Cent. quarters of Milan lead into this street; the fourth to the left is via Sant'Andrea where at no. 6 we find the *Palazzo Morando Attendolo Bolognini* of the XVIIIth Cent., which contains the *Civic*

Palazzo dei Giureconsulti.

Museum of Contemporary History inaugurated in 1963 and the *Milan Museum* founded in 1935. Via Monte Napoleone leads into Corso Matteotti to the right, and the lively piazza San Babila to the left which is the meeting point for several important roads. It is surrounded by modern high buildings with porticos and at the end the *Column of the Lion* (Colonna del Leone) (1626) and on the right of the square, the Basilica of San Babila of the XIth Cent. but much altered since Alessandro Manzoni was baptized in this church on the 8th August 1785, as the plaque commemorates. We continue, along Corso Vittorio Emanuele which was almost totally reconstructed after the damage suffered during the war. It is full of life with porticos on either side and luxury shops of various kinds and cafès. This street leads to the northern side of Piazza del Duomo. After the Northern porticoed Arcade, we take via Mercanti, flanked on the right by **Palazzo dei Giureconsulti** built in 1562 by the architect Vincenzo Seregni for Pope Pius IV (Angelo Maria Medici, who was a Milanese). The façade was designed by Galeazzo Alessi. The building which has a stepped base, a twin-columned portico, richly windows and a tower built in 1272. The statue on the ground floor of *St. Ambrose* by Luigi Scorzini replaces the original statue of Philip II which was transformed into Brutus during the French Revolution. On the

39

The Arches of Porta Nuova. - Roman busts on the inner façade.

other side lies the **Palazzo della Ragione** (Palace of Reason) or **Broletto Nuovo**, the most remarkable building of the Free Commune period, in Romanesque Style. It was built in 1233, its ground floor was raised, and it is open with archways upon pillars and three-mullioned windows on the first floor; in 1771 a second floor was added. On the side which looks onto the piazza, there is a Romanesque high-relief which shows the first podestà of Milan Oldrado da Tresseno, by Benedetto Antelami (1233) The picturesque **Piazza Mercanti** which originally formed a closed quadrangle was once the true heart of mediaeval Milan and even to-day is surrounded by many important monuments. In front of the

Detail of the façade of the Loggia of the Osii.

Palazzo della Ragione there is the **Palazzo delle Scuole Palatine** (Palace of the Palatine Schools) built in 1645 by Carlo Buzzi who used the architectural motifs of the Palazzo dei Giureconsulti. The statue above the arch, shows the poet Ausonius (died 394) who wrote verses in praise of Milan. To the left of the palazzo, the **Loggia degli Osii** which Matteo Visconti had built in 1316 by Scoto da S. Gemignano. It is all in black and white marble, with two loggias one on top of the other. The upper part is decorated with graceful three-mullioned niches which contain nine XIVth Cent. statues of the *Madonna and Saints*. Along the parapet of the upper loggia are to be seen the arms and devices of the Viscontis.

Going towards the Castello Sforzesco

At the northern corner of Piazza del Duomo, where the Northern Arcade ends, one takes via dei Mercanti which is flanked to the right by Palazzo dei Giureconsulti and to the left by Palazzo della Ragione. The road ends in Piazza Cordusio, at the centre of which rises the bronze *Monument to Giuseppe Parini* by Luigi Secchi (1899). After having crossed the square, we go straight down via Dante, one of the most lively thoroughfares of the city with its large buildings, to which the Castle Tower acts as a back-drop. The street ends in Largo Cairoli with the *Monument to Giuseppe Garibaldi* by Ettore Ximenes (1895) in the middle. To the right and left of Largo Cairoli large avenues lined with trees begin, forming a semi-circle around the Sforzesco Castle and known as Foro Buonaparte. From behind the monument via Beltrami leads to the grand Castle square (piazza Castello) with flower beds and trees.

CASTELLO SFORZESCO

The castle, which is one of the greatest monuments of the Renaissance period, was started in the XIVth Cent., when Galeazzo II Visconti ordered building to begin on a stronghold and the name of *Castle of the Jovian Gate* was given to it since it was in the vicinity of Porta Giovia (the Jovian Gate of the Roman wall). It also incorporated a part of the wall in its structure. It was then extended by his successors, Gian Galeazzo, Giovanni Maria and finally by Filippo Maria, who had it altered and improved with the help of the architect Filippo Brunelleschi, as he wished it to be used as the permanent residence of the Visconti dynasty. After the death of Duke Filippo Maria (1447) the stronghold was sacked by the Ambrosian Republic which had taken over the government of the city. In 1450, the soldier of fortune (Condottiero) Francesco Sforza, after the fall of the republic, took possession of the stronghold. He began the reconstruction with the intention of creating a fortification for his own defence but it was gradually transformed into an architecturally impressive noble residence. To start with, the work was entrusted to Giovanni da Milano with the assistance of Filippo Scorzioli and in 1451 the direction of the works passed to Jacopo da Cortona. In 1452 the Prince engaged the Florentine architect Filarete to construct and decorate the middle tower of the castle which however was begun two years later, when work on the building under the direction of Bar-

Bird's-eye view of the Castello Sforzesco.

tolomeo Gadio of Cremona resumed. After the death of Francesco Sforza (1466) his son Galeazzo Maria succeeded him and had the work continued under the architect Benedetto Ferrigni, also from Florence, to whom we owe the loggia, the great staircase of honour, the portico of the Elephant, the chapel and the rear end of the Rocchetta. The decoration was entrusted to painters of the Dukedom. Under the regency of Bona di Savoia, the tower was built to which she gave her name (1476). With the rise to power of Ludovico il Moro (1494) the fourth son of Francesco Sforza, the castle became one of the most splendid residences, decorated by Bramante, the great Leonardo da Vinci and numerous other artists summoned to work there. After Ludovico il Moro's fall (1499), the magnificent palace was occupied by the French forces commanded by marshal Gian Giacomo Trivulzio and the beginning of the destruction of the splendid castle commenced. In 1521, a gun powder explosion caused the destruction of the central tower built by Filarete. During the Spanish domination (XVIth- XVIIth Cent.) the castle underwent further transformation and addition of buildings, becoming a military fortress. Charles V had a new rampart built which connected it to the new walls of the city; at the end of the XVIth Cent. the stronghold was surrounded by six bulwarks; at the beginning of the XVIth Cent. the moat was put in order and the covered road along the external border, and

43

Castello Sforzesco. - The façade with the Tower of Filarete.

six detached ravelins were built. In 1707 the Spaniards finally capitulated to General Koenigseck. In 1733, the fortress was conquered by Charles Emmanuel III of Savoy at the head of the Franco-Sardinian troops. In 1746 the fortress was once more reconquered by the Spaniards for a short time. In 1796 it was conquered by the French and in 1799 by Suvaroff. After the Austrians had abandoned the fortress, Napoleon demolished the Spanish additions and only the original Castello Sforzesco was left standing. In 1814 the Austrians returned and during the "five days" of March 1845 Radetsky withdrew into the Castle with his general staff and his troops and from here bombarded the city

Castello Sforzesco. - The drawbridge (detail).

and ordered the demolition of the corner towers. With the liberation of Lombardy the old castle became a barracks and in 1880 was sentenced to complete destruction. During the following years, however, a large number of Milanese and the interest of the Lombard Historical Society foiled all attempts in this direction, so much so that in 1893 the architect Luca Beltrami, who had already put foward a project, began a radical reconstruction. In the three nuclei of the historical building - the Parade Ground, the Rocchetta and the Ducal Court he sited the Civic Institute for Art and History. Although it was damaged once more during the last war, the Sforza Castle was restored and became a Museum.

Castello Sforzesco. - The Castle seen from the Sempione Park.
Right: **the Tower of Filarete, frontal view.**

THE CASTLE EXTERIOR.. - At the centre of the façade with its front towards the city rises the so-called *Filarete Tower* (called also the *Clock Tower*) (dell'Orologio) which is 70 metres high. It was reconstructed at the beginning of this century by the architect Luca Beltrami, and was given back the appearance it had had before the destruction of 1561. It is quadrangular in shape with two upper storeys, each one narrower than the lower, culminating in a small cupola. Above the great door is a bas-relief by Luigi Secchi representing *King Umberto II* on horseback (1916). Higher-up, under the first battlements is *St. Ambrose* amidst the coats of arms of the six Sforza dukes. Six magnificently ornamented and richly decorated marble and brick mullioned windows are set into the powerfully structured front walls of the castle, which stretch out left and right from the Central Clock tower, leading to the two massive cylindrical corner towers dressed in rough-hewn blocks of stone. They are 31 metres high, crowned with battlements and decorated with the great marble coat of arms with the Visconti-Sforza grass-snake. The sides and the rear have the same characteristics as the façade and at the level of the Rocchetta and the Ducal Court are two series of large gothic windows decorated with brickwork frames. The corner towers at the back are called *Torre Falconiera* to the right and *Torre Castellana* (or of the *Treasure*) to the left; they are square with large windows. At the centre of the side facing the Park there is the great *Porta del Barco*. On the left side, next to *Porta Santo Spirito*, picturesque restored ruins of a ravelin. On the right is the *Porta dei Carmini* with a drawbridge and the bridge of Ludovico il Moro.

47

THE INTERIOR. - The doorway, under the tower of Filarete, leads into the grand and picturesque **Parade Ground** (Piazza d'Armi), now a garden, was once used to exercise the Sforza troops. The internal front of the tower is distinguished by a balcony with a three-mullioned window, whilst along the left side of the wall runs a construction which acts as a support. The bottom of the courtyard is closed by three buildings with a *dry moat* in front of them; to the left stands the **Rocchetta**, a fortified building in which the Sforzas took refuge in dangerous moments; almost at the centre stands the Tower of **Bona di Savoia** 36 metres high and commissioned by the widow of Galeazzo Maria Sforza in 1477; to the right, the palace of the **Ducal Court**, the residence of the Sforzas in times of peace and tranquillity. The solitary statue in front of the moat is *St. John Nepomucenus* erected in 1729. At the sides of the great square two doors with a drawbridge that crosses the external moat; the right one is *Porta dei Carmini* decorated with architectural fragments of different epochs; the left one is the *Porta di Santo Spirito* (Door of the Holy Spirit).

THE DUCAL COURT. - The access is through the door surmounted by a great Sforza coat of arms, which rises upon the site of the old Jovian Gate and leads into the **Vestibule** where sculptures and fragments of various Milanese buildings are kept. On the wall one can still see the fresco of the *Crucifix between Saints* by an unknown Lombard (1470-80) showing the sponsor, Ambrosino da Longhignana, who was at that time the keeper of the castle for Galeazzo Maria Sforza and Bona di Savoia. From the vestibule one enters the stupendous **Courtyard** of the Ducal Court, flanked on three sides by a two storey construction with two rows of ogival windows. The ground floor of the end wall is graced by the Renaissance "Elephant" Door, which owes its name to the frescoed Elephant on the wall, by Benedetto Ferrini (1473) who also designed the two-storeyed graceful loggia at the beginning of the left wing, called the *Loggia of Galeazzo Maria*, that stands above the vestibule of the great staircase.

Castello Sforzesco. - Left and above: **the Great Courtyard or Parade Ground.** Below: **the courtyard of the Ducal Court.**

The Art Museums. - One enters the museums from the right wing of the courtyard. The setting, in the framework of the ancient rooms, including the collections of sculptures, paintings, furniture and tapestries, musical instruments, works of art in gold, ivory, glass and pottery etc. has been renovated according to modern standards. On the ground floor we find the Sculpture Museum, prevalently Lombard, which begins with some examples of late Roman Empire and Byzantine art. On the upper floor there is a collection of furniture with examples which range from the late Gothic chests of the XVth Cent. The Picture Gallery with its prevalently Lombard works, boasts a variety of paintings by great artists of various epochs. In the rooms of the Rocchetta, pottery, gold, bronzes, ivory, wrought iron and glass are displayed. In addition there also exists the Museum of Ancient Musical Instruments, which is a unique collection in Europe. A list of the most interesting items in the 32 rooms follows.

ROOM 1. - (Early Christian and pre-Romanesque art). - Past the entrance and before entering the Museum, we find the *Blacksmith's Postern* which belonged to the XIVth Cent. Visconti wall. Here are displayed fragments of mosaic floors, frescœs from tombs, various architectural fragments, capitals, sarcophagi, sculptures etc.; which date from the IVth to the IXth Cent. Of interest: fragment of *Early Christian sarcophagus* with male and female figures of the IVth Cent.; a fresco from a tomb with a *bejewelled Cross and deer* of the VIth Cent., from the church of S. Giovanni in Conca; head in marble, perhaps of the empress *Theodora* of the VIth Cent.; *fragment of a head* from the Baptistery of St. John in Florence.

ROOM 2. - (Romanesque and Campionese art.). - This room is dominated by the *Sepulcral Monument and Equestrian Statue of Bernabò Visconti*, from the church of S. Giovanni in Conca. The equestrian statue is by Bonito da Campione (1370-80). On the walls are reliefs and fragments of the XIIth Cent.; wooden *Crucifix* of the XIIIth Cent.; relief of *Christ Blessing*; *Sarcophagus of Giovanni da Fagnano*; the front of the *sarcophagus of Vieri da Bassignana* of the XIVth Cent.; *the sepulchral*'*monument of Regina della Scala* the wife of Bernabò Visconti, of the XIVth Cent. In the lunettes and on the wall at the end we find various coats of arms of Spanish governors.

ROOM 3. - The fresco on the vault representing the *Resurrection* is by an unknown XVth Cent. Lombard artist. The borders of the vaults are decorated with coats of arms of the dukedom. Along the wall is the *statue of St. James the Elder* of the XIVth Cent.; the front of the sarcophagus of *brother Mirano di Bechaloe,* Campionese art; statue of *Madonna and Child* and *St. Ambrose* which decorated the tabernacles of the Porta Comacina, a *Madonna between Saints Babila, Ambrose, Benedict and Dionysius* which once decorated the Eastern Door, works of the school of Giovanni Balduccio of Pisa. The *slab from the tomb of Bona di Savoia* of the XVth Cent. and another *slab from the tomb of Antonello Arcimboldi* (1438). Interesting also, in the middle of the room, the almond-shaped upper decoration of a window with the *Redeemer* and the *Assumption*, by a XIVth Cent. Tuscan master.

ROOM 4. - The vault is decorated with the great heraldic coat of arms of Philip II King of Spain and his wife Mary Tudor (1555). On the walls a XIVth Cent. *Madonna*; slab with *Deposition*, Campionese art; architectural remains and fragments of the façade of the church of S. Maria di Brera, by Giovanni di Balduccio of Pisa, of the XIVth Cent.; *Tabernacle*, the work of a Burgundy master; *Sepulchral monument of the Rusca family*, by a

Castello Sforzesco (Museum). - Monument and equestrian statue of Bernabò Visconti, by Bonino da Campione.

Lombard master of the XIVth Cent. The fresco on the left wall with the *Annunciation* is of the XIVth Cent. from San Giovanni in Conca.

ROOM 5. - The *Headless Madonna*, a small statue by Giovanni Pisano of the XIVth Cent. is here, with the *Kiss of Judas*, an alabaster relief by a XIVth Cent. English artist; Venetian sculpture of the XVth Cent. and on the floor a *slab from the tomb of Giovanni Lanfranchi* of the XIVth Cent.

ROOM 6. - Devoted to the historical remains of Milan amongst which the bas-reliefs representing the *Return of the Milanese to Milan* after the sack of Barbarossa and *St. Ambrose chasing out the Arians* from the now demolished Porta Romana by Anselmo and Gherardo da Campione (1171).

ROOM 7. - On the walls are Mantuan tapestries, and some of the Flemish school of the XVIIIth Cent.; at the centre of the room is the rich *standard of the city* of 1566, by Giuseppe Meda. The figures at the two sides, embroidered in silk, gold and silver with painted parts, represent episodes in the life of St. Ambrose and Italian coats of arms. In addition Renaissance sculptures amongst which the statue of *Adam* by Stoldo Lorenzi; the bust in marble of *Ottavio Farnese* and busts of *Roman Emperors*.

ROOM 8. - This room is called *Room of the wooden planks* because in the time of Galeazzo Maria Sforza the lower sections of the walls were covered with wooden wainscoating. But the importance of this room lies in the decorations by Leonardo (1498) all around the walls, which are painted with tree trunks with heavy foliage which converges in the centre of the vault where the coat of arms of Ludovico il Moro is frescoed. The tiny door in the right wall leads to the *Bridge of Ludovico il Moro* by Bramante.

ROOM 9. - It is also known as the *Black room* because Ludovico il Moro used to retreat here in meditation after the death of his wife Beatrice D'Este. It is said that this room was originally decorated by Leonardo. Along the walls in the lunettes, are medallions with *Portraits of the Sforzas* executed by Bernardino Luini, from the Atellani houses. In addition there are sculptures of the XVIth Cent. by Bambaia which decorated the tomb of Birago, in the church of San Francesco Grande.

ROOM 10. - In this small room the series of portraits of the Sforzas continues: also Lombard and Tuscan Sculptures of the XVIth Cent.

ROOM 11. - Known also as *Room of the Dukes* because of the coats of arms of the Sforza dynasty painted on the vault against a blue background, which bear the initials of Galeazzo Maria Sforza. At the time of the Dukedom it was an audience hall. Between the various sculptures, the slab with *Allegorical Scene* by Agostino di Duccio, which comes from the Malatesta Temple in Rimini, is the most interesting.

ROOM 12. - The ducal chapel was decorated in 1466-76 by Stefano de' Fedeli and assistants by order of Galeazzo Maria Sforza. On the vault *Resurrection*; in the lunettes the *Annunciation* and coats of arms; along the walls, *Saints*. In the centre of the room, statue known as the *Coazzone* or *Praying Madonna*, a work attributed to Pietro Solari. In addition, *Madonna and Child* on a small pedestal supported by cherubs and Angel, Gothic art of the XVth Cent. Also *Angel Musicians* in the style of Amadeo.

ROOM 13. - Known also as the *Sala delle Colombine* (Doves) on account of its frescoes of gold tondi with doves against a red background, which Bona di Savoia had painted. Amongst the various Lombard sculptures are

Castello Sforzesco (Museum). - **Rondanini Pietà by Michelangelo.**

Angels and Anchorites by Cristofaro Mantegazza and *Angels* by Amadeo. The two portals of the XVth Cent., facing each other are also interesting.

ROOM 14. - Known as the *Green Room* because it was originally painted green. Here one finds Renaissance portals amongst which the magnificent marble one, *Portal of the Banco Mediceo* by the Florentine Michelozzo (1455) is of major interest. In addition the Orsini- Roma portal of the XVIth Cent.; the *Bentivoglio Portal* of the XVIth Cent.; *capitals of the Portico of Figini* of the XVth Cent. which come from Piazza del Duomo are worthy of note. In the glass case are Longobard and Renaissance arms, and Italian and German armour of the XVIth Cent.

ROOM 15. - Known as the *Room of the Scarlioni* on account of the arrow-like stripes painted in red on the wall, of which only traces remain. Here the secret counsels were held and it was also used as an audience hall. The room is divided into two parts; in the first one the *statue of Gaston de Foix, lying in death,* by Bambaia whose brother also co-operated in the enterprise until 1525, and the *great funeral monument of the Bishop Bagaroto* by Andrea Fusina (1519). In the second part a staircase leads to a niche shrining the famous *Pietà Rondanini* by Michelangelo, last work his.

One leaves this rooms through a small door at the end and crosses the *Courtyard of the Fountain* by means of a wooden gallery. In the courtyard, a copy of the ancient marble fountain of the Sforzas (the original is in the cathedral of Bellinzona). To the right, the staircase, also known as the Stair of the Small Horse (Scala Cavallina) leads to the floor above.

ROOM 16. - Known also as *Upper Green Room* where the great receptions were held in the time of the dukedom. This room is divided into four completely independent compartments. One enters the three following compartments through the next rooms. Amongst the many things in the first compartment are: the inlaid *Tower Chest*, of the XVth Cent.; a very rare wooden *Booth* called *Coretto* by Torrechiara, XVth Cent. Amongst the frescoes on the walls we note the *Crucifixion.*

ROOM 17. - As well as furniture, this room contains an important series of frescoes of the Lombard school. *Allegorical figures* of the XV-XVIth Cents. and *Episodes from the life of Jesus* of the XVIth Cent. In the centre is a remarkable attempt to reconstruct the frescoes of the *Stories of Griselda* from the castle of Roccabianca, a work attributed to Nicolò da Varallo. From here one enters the two compartments of Room 16, where chests, beds, chests of drawers are exhibited with cupboards, caskets. Upon a great Tuscan table of the XVIIth Cent. stands a basin of chiselled and cast bronze, a beautiful work by Leone Leoni.

ROOM 18. - Among the numerous paintings on the walls are *Spring* by Gerolamo da Ponte; *the Forge of Vulcan* which tradition has, was completed in a single night by Morazzone by candlelight; the *Holy Family* by Danilo Crespi. The most precious of the pieces of furniture is the celebrated *Passalacqua Casket* of 1613, its beautiful design embellished with ivory, bronze, and paintings by Morazzone. From here one enters the last compartment of room 16, with Venetian furniture of the XVIIIth Cent. and two sedan chairs one of which is Neopolitan and richly decorated. On the walls are paintings including the *Procession of the Imperial Ambassador Clerici* by the Florentine, Antonio Cioci (1759) and *Portrait of a great Lady* attributed to Alessandro Longhi.

ROOM 19. - This room contains furniture of the XVIIIth Cent. from various places. Of great interest is the Piedmontese chest of drawers with a Viennese clock on it; the four Lombard chairs are covered with tapestry

Castello Sforzesco (Museum). - **Stories of Griselda** (detail from the cycle of frescoes from the Castle of Roccabianca).

upholstery and the chest of drawers is decorated in bronze with a marble group upon it representing *Aeneas, Anchises and Ascanius*.

ROOM 20. - This room, known also as the *Golden Room*, and the following six rooms contain the Picture Gallery. Among the many works on display here of the various schools of the XIV-XVth Cents. the following are particularly interesting: *Madonna and Child between Saints and Angels* by Filippo Lippi; Madonna and Child by Giovanni Bellini and *Poet Laureate* also attributed to him. The great tempera in the middle of the room of the *Madonna in Glory among Saints* is by Andrea Mantegna (1497).

ROOM 21.- Dedicated to the Lombard painters of the XV-XVIth Cents. By Bergognone there is a *Deposition, St. Benedict giving Alms, St. Jerome* and *St. Roch.* By Foppa: *two Holy Bishops*, the famous *St. Sebastian*, the *Madonna of the book*, the *Madonna Trivulzio, St. Francis* and *St. John the Baptist.* Also: the *Madonna* by Bernardino Luini; *Portrait of a woman*, by Boltraffio; *St. Michael* by Sodoma and other works by Romanino Moretto, Bramantino, De Predis and others.

ROOM 22. - This little hall contains a number of small Mannerist paintings.

ROOM 23. - Lombard paintings from the Chapel of the Tribunale di Provvisione (the town's main administrative organ). Works by Salmeggia,

Nuvolone, Figino, etc. and a very interesting *Pentecost* by Morazzone.

ROOM 24. - Italian Mannerists of Northern Italy. A particularly fine *Martyrdom of St. Sebastian* by A. Campi (1575) and various works by Procaccini. The *Door* adorned with crests and medallions comes from the house that was given to Lucia Marliani by Galeazzo Maria Sforza in 1474.

ROOM 25. - The Lombard Region Room. - Works normally stored in the Museum deposits take turns in being exhibited in this room.

ROOM 26. - XVIIth and XVIIIth Cent. paintings. The Lombard works are separated from the other schools. Of particular interest: *St. Michael Archangel* by Cerano, *St. Charles fasting* by Danilo Crespi, *two Storms* by Magnasco, *Portrait of a Young Man* by Fra Galgario, *St. Francis in Extasy* by Francesco del Cairo, *Storm at Sea* by F. Guardi.

The small door at the end of the great hall leads to a small bridge which crosses the high part of the Tower of Bona di Savoia, and leads eventually to the rooms on the upper floor of the Rocchetta, where the pottery, gold and ivory etc. are displayed. Past rooms 27 and 28 (the latter contains wrought iron objects) is the enormous **Pottery Section** which occupies three rooms. In the first (29) one finds decorative and figurative pottery and even examples of pottery graffiti. In the second room (30) which is divided into compartments, the statues attributed to Giovanni di Balduccio da Pisa and the portraits of personalities from the Visconti and Sforza families are interesting. The Chinese pottery, the pottery of Faenza of the XVth to XVIIth Cents., that of Urbino, Savona, Albisola, Angarano, Castelli d'Abruzzo and the pottery of Milan and Lodi in the glass cases, are all worthy of note. in the third room (31) there are examples of Italian and foreign pottery of the XVIII-XIXth Cents. Also pottery from Vienna, Doccia, Capodimonte, Meissen, Venice and Sèvres. The 32nd room is devoted to gold, ivory and bronze objects. Amongst these, the Gothic *Monstrance* of 1456, the XVIth Cent. *Stories of the Passion*, and the two beautiful caravels are the most interesting. Among the ivory works are the famous tablets with the *Two Marys at the Sepulchre*, Roman art of the Vth Cent., and the diptych of the *Console Magno*, Byzantine art of the VIth Cent; precious Murano glass and various bronze objects of interest.

The rooms of the lower floor around the Rocchetta are devoted to Hellenistic and Coptic textiles of the IInd to VIIIth Cents., and to liturgical hangings, costumes etc., and to the *Museum of Ancient Musical Instruments* founded in 1958 and opened to the public in 1963. This collection of 641 pieces can be considered the only one of its kind in Europe. It contains string, plucked, keyboard and wind instruments arranged in such a way as to give an idea of the history of musical instruments over five centuries, from the XVth Cent. to modern times. All the instruments are of great interest either because they are works of great masters such as Gasparo da Salò, Guarnieri, or Stradivari, or on account of their great artistic value. On the same floor there is the **Room of the Ball** (Sala della Balla) normally closed since it is reserved for receptions or ceremonies) where the famous 12 tapestries with the allegories of the *Months* made for Marshal Trivulzio in 1503 (to designs by Bramantino), by the ducal tapestry weavers of Vigevano hang.

THE COURTYARD OF THE ROCCHETTA. - Access to this down the great severe staircase. The Rocchetta is a fortress within a fortress surrounded on three sides by porticoes; the right one was constructed by the Florentine Benedetto Ferrini (1466-76) by order of Gian Galeazzo Maria, the one opposite is by Filarete and the left one was begun by Bernardino da Corte in 1495 and finished by Bramante under the orders of Ludovico il Moro.

Castello Sforzesco. - The Rocchetta Courtyard.

From the Courtyard, through an archway, one enters the **Treasure Room**, so called, because the ducal treasure was kept there, with frescoes of the Lombard school and a damaged fresco by Bramante on one of the walls, showing Argus with a hundred eyes guarding the door leading to a small room in which the most precious jewels of the Duke were kept.

Leaving the Castle by the *Porta del Barco* across the moat, the **Park** lies directly ahead. It is a vast garden in the English style which takes up an area of 47 hectares with picturesque groups of trees, green lawns and flower beds. In the background we see the **Arch of Peace** (Arco della Pace). To the right we take via Gadio to get to the **Civic Aquarium** and behind at the edge of the park is the **Arena or Civic Stadium** an elliptical neoclassical construction attributed to Luigi Canonica and inaugurated in 1807 in the presence of Napoleon. In the arena, which nowadays is reserved for competitive sports, horse racing and curricle races were once held. Within the boundaries of the park there is also the **Palazzo dell'Arte** (the palace of art) the permanent seat of the exhibition of decorative arts (Triennale) which takes place every three years. On the small hill known as the *Monte Tondo* (round mount) rises the monument to *Napoleon III* by Francesco Bazagli (1881). Spacious Piazza Sempione lies on the other side of the park.

The Arch of Peace (Arco della Pace).

THE ARCH OF PEACE

Is one of the most typical monuments of Milan. It is by the neoclassical artist, Luigi Cagnola to celebrate the exploits of Napoleon, an intention somewhat foiled by subsequent events. It was begun in 1807 and in 1826 the monument was dedicated to Francis I of Austria and called the Arch of Peace to commemorate the Peace of Europe in 1815. Successively, in 1859, it was used to commemorate the entry of Victor Emmanuel II and Napoleon III into Milan. The monument which is 25 metres high, is composed of 3 arches with 4 columns which protrude at the front and is surmounted by the great bronze *Peace Chariot drawn by six horses* by Abbondio Sangiorgio while the *Four Victories* on horseback at the corners are by Giovanni Patti. Above the trabeation, the four principal rivers of Lombardy and the Veneto are represented: the Po, the Ticino, the Adige and the Tagliamento. The reliefs on the two façades show episodes of the Restoration after the fall of Napoleon.

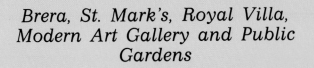

Brera, St. Mark's, Royal Villa, Modern Art Gallery and Public Gardens

Brera Palace.

To get to the Brera Art Gallery it is best to begin from Piazza della Scala, taking via Giuseppe Verdi where one sees the elegant baroque façade of the **church of San Giuseppe** on the right, one of the finest architectural achievements of Francesco M. Richini (1630). The road continues until is gets to via Brera, a typical Milanese street, flanked by neoclassical and XVIIIth Cent. palaces amongst which to the left, at no. 15 is the *Cusani Palace* by Giovanni Ruggeri (1719). On the right, at no. 28 lies the *Brera Palace*.

THE BRERA PALACE

Brera. - The magnificent courtyard.

This monumental building was built by the Jesuits on the site of a pre-existing monastery of the Humiliated Brethren. The job of constructing this palace was given to Francesco Maria Richini, who worked on the project from 1651 until his death in 1658. His son Gian Domenico continued working on the project and others followed until it was finally completed in 1773. The great portal was added in 1780 by Piermarini. The entrance hall leads into a superb rectangular courtyard with two rows of arches supported by twin columns which is Richini's masterpiece based upon designs by Martino Bassi. At the centre of the courtyard is a bronze statue of Napoleon I, by Antonio Canova (1809). The emperor bears the simbol of victory in his right hand and the sceptre of command in his left hand. Statues and busts representing illustrious personalities of the arts and sciences who took part in the life of Milan, are to be found between the surrounding columns. After the suppression of the Jesuit order which occurred in 1772 the Empress Marie Theresa of Austria assigned the palace to various institutions and even to-day it is the seat of the Academy of Fine Arts, the National Library, the Astronomical Observatory, and the Picture Gallery.

THE BRERA ART GALLERY

Brera. - Jesus in the Garden, by Veronese.

It was conceived in 1776 as the teaching section of the Academy, was promoted to the status of National Gallery during the Napoleonic period and on the 15th of August 1809 it opened its rooms with the intention of stimulating the interest of the wider public in the arts. From a nucleus of modest works which existed at first, it has become, with the passing of time, one of the most important galleries in Italy. The collection is composed, for the most part, of works confiscated by the state between the end of the XVIIIth Cent. and the beginning of the XIXth Cent. following the suppression of various religious orders, and also of donations and acquisitions. To-day, the thirty-eight rooms contain examples of all the Italian schools, prevalently of the Lombard and Venetian ones, as well as a considerable number of foreign works. The picture gallery which was badly hit during the bomb attacks during the war, has been completely reconstructed and is now arranged in accordance with the latest museum criteria.

ROOM 1. or FRESCO GALLERY. - Lombard school of the XV-XVIth Cents. *Madonna and Child between St. John the Baptist and St. John the Evangel-*

61

58

ist and *Martyrdom of St. Sebastian* by Vincenzo Foppa (1485) both come from the church of S. Maria di Brera; *Madonna and child with Angels* from the church of S. Maria dei Servi; the *Adoration of the Magi* and *Stories of St. Anne and of the Madonna*, the last works of Gaudenzio Ferrari (1545) from the church of S. Maria della Pace. Also, series of frescoes by Bernardino Luini (1520-25) from the Villa Pelucca, amongst which the *Gathering of the Manna* the *Remains of St. Catherine transported by Angels*, and *Venus and Adonis*.

ROOM 2. - The chapel of Mocchirolo is reconstructed in its original form in this room, with a series of Lombard frescoes of the XIVth Cent., attributed to Giovanni da Milano. The magnificent frescoes represent the *Crucifixion, Christ amongst the symbols of the Evangelists, Count Porra with his family* shows the model of the chapel to the Madonna; *St. Ambrose scourges the heretics* and the *Mystic Wedding of St. Catherine*. There is also a Sienese masterpiece by Ambrogio Lorenzetti, *the Madonna and Child*.

ROOM 3. - Devoted to Venetian and Lombard painters of the XVIth Cent. *Madonna in glory and St. Jerome, St. Francis and St. Anthony Abbot* and *Madonna between St. Paul, St. Jerome, St. Catherine of Alexandria and St. Clare* two works by Moretto; *Madonna in glory and Saints* by Girolamo Savoldo; *St. Sebastian, St. Helen, St. Roch* and *St. Constantine* by Palma

63

Brera. - The Sermon of St. Mark in Alexandria (detail), **by Giovanni and Gentile Bellini.**

the Elder; *Portrait of Antonio Navagero* by Gian Battista Moroni; *Deposition* by Lorenzo Lotto; *the Last Supper* and *Jesus in the garden* by Paolo Veronese.

ROOM 4. - Venetian masters of the XVIth Cent.. There are five works by Tintoretto including *Christ taken from the Cross* and *the Finding of the body of Saint Mark.* Two masterpieces by Paolo Veronese: *Supper in the house of the Pharisee* and *St. Anthony Abbot between Saints Cornelius and Cyprian. Portrait of Febo da Brescia* and *Portrait of Laura da Pola* by Lorenzo Lotto and other works by Palma the Younger, Bassano, Bonifacio Veronese and Paris Bordone.

ROOM 5. - Dedicated to Venetian artists of the XV-XVIth Cents. This room contains Gentile Bellini's marvellous *Sermon of St. Mark in Alexandria in Egypt* finished by his brother Giovanni; *Madonna on the throne and Saints* by Bartolomeo Montagna; *Coronation of the Virgin* by Andrea Previtale; *Madonna on the Throne and Saints* and *St. Peter the Martyr between St. Nicolas of Bari and St. Augustine* by Giovan Battista Cima and other works by Liberale da Verona, Martino da Udine, Marco Basaiti, Cariani, Alvise Vivarini, also the Artists' Self-Portraits Cabinet, with portraits of Nuvolone, Palma the Younger, Ferretti, Hayez, etc.

ROOM 6. - Dedicated to Donato Bramante, the frescoes from Palazzo Panigerola are all assembled here, e.g.: the *Man at arms*, the *Cantor*, *Heraclitus* and *Democritus* and a remarkable *Christ at the Column.*

ROOM 8. - Devoted to Venetians of the XVth Cent.: *Madonna and Saints* by Cima da Conegliano, a *Poliptych* and The *Dead Christ* by Andrea Mantegna; *Madonna of the little Candle, Coronation of Mary and Saints*

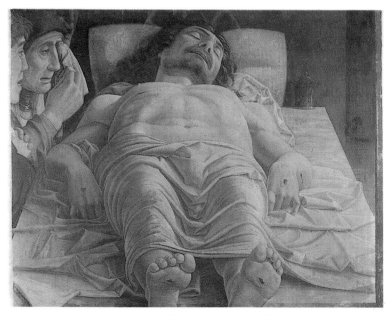

Brera. - The Dead Christ, by Andrea Mantegna.

and other works by Carlo Crivelli, the *Madonna and Child* and the powerful *Lamentation over the dead Christ*, by Giovanni Bellini. Also, the *Dispute of St. Stephen* by Vittore Carpaccio and *St. Jerome* by Cima da Conegliano. Also works by Lorenzetti and Gentile da Fabriano.

ROOMS 7-9-14. - Lombard and Piedmontese painters of the XVth and XVIth Cents. Admirable *Tryptych* showing *Madonna and Child with Saints Leonard and Bernardino*, by Butinone, *Madonna and Child, The Doctors of the Church, Ludovico il Moro* by *The Master* of the Sforza Altarpiece; *Portrait of a Young Man* by Andrea Solario; *Madonna and Child* by Bramantino; *Madonna and Child* by Cesare da Sesto.

ROOMS 15-16. - Devoted to the works of Bernardino Luini. The frescoes from the church of Santa Maria della Pace, representing *Episodes in the life of Mary and St. Joseph*, in their original order. In addition by Luini, the *Madonna and Child between Saints John and Martha.*

ROOM 17. - Dedicated to Lombard painters of the XV-XVIth Cents. The *Annunciation* by Bernardino Luini; the *Archangels overcome the devil* by Marco D'Oggiono; the *Presentation at the Temple* by Romanino; the *Martyrdom of St. Catherine* by Gaudenzio Ferrari, *Crucifixion* by Bramantino; poliptych with *Madonna and Saints* and *Annunciation, Visitation, Nativity* and the *Flight into Egypt* on the predella by Vincenzo Foppa; the *Coronation of Mary* and *Saints Ambrose, Jerome and Catherine* with *Lamentation over the Dead Christ* in the lunette, both by Bergognone.

ROOM 18. - Dedicated to Andrea Mantegna and Carlo Crivelli. Notice the unusual perspective used by Mantegna in his *Dead Christ* as well as his *St. Luke the Evangelist and Saints*. See also a *Crucifixion*, the *Madonna of*

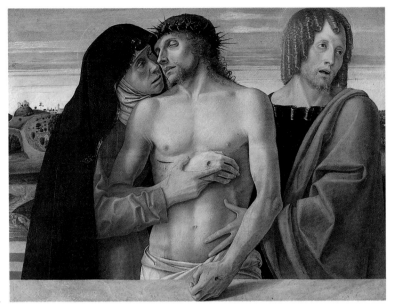

Brera. - Pietà, by Giovanni Bellini.

the little Candle (della Candeletta), the *Coronation of the Virgin* and a gigantic *Dead Christ* painted for the Church of St. Francis in Fabriano.

ROOM 19. - Venetian painters of the XVth Cents. The *Redeemer with Hand raised in Blessing* by A. Vivarini, *The Virgin presented at the Temple* and *St. Stephen and the Disputants* by Vittore Carpaccio. Two *Madonnas* and a *Deposition* (Pietà) by Giovanni Bellini, a *Madonna and Child* by Antonello da Messina.

ROOM 20. - Devoted to Emilian painters of the XVIth Cent. *Nativity and Adoration of the Magi* both by the young Correggio; *St. Peter and the Baptist* by Francesco del Cossa; fragments of a *Crucifix* by Cosmè Tura; *St. George, St. John the Baptist and St. Sebastian* by Dosso Dossi and other works by Lorenzo Costa, Gian Francesco Maineri, Filippo Mazzola.

ROOMS 21-22-23. - Works from the deposits take turns in being exhibited in Room 22 alone, as the other two are used for storing works of art.

ROOMS 24-25-26. - These rooms have recently been restructured and are dedicated to the works of Piero della Francesca and Raphael. The *Madonna and Child, Angels, Saints and Federico da Montefeltro* by Piero della Francesca, from the Church of St. Bernardino in Urbino, was commissioned by the Duke to celebrate the birth of his son Guidobaldo. Raphael's *Espousal of the Virgin*, painted in Città di Castello in 1504. Other paintings by Bramante, Luca Signorelli and others.

ROOM 27. - *Madonna and Saints*, a *Madonna* and *the Flagellation* three works by Luca Signorelli, *Andrea Doria in the guise of Neptune* by Bronzino; *Madonna and Child and Saints* by Timoteo Viti; the same subject by Gerolamo Genga and other works by Pedro Berruguete.

Brera. - Espousal of the Virgin, by Raphael.

ROOM 28. - Reserved to Bolognese painters of the XVI-XVIIIth Cents. The *Martyrdom of St. Vitalius* by Barocci, *the Adoration of the Magi* and the *Woman of Canaan* works by Ludovico Carracci; *Saints Peter and Paul* by Guido Reni and other works by Lucio Massari and Annibale Carracci.

ROOM 29. - Italian XVIIth Cent. painters in this and the following room. The *Martyrs Valerian, Tiburzius and Cecilia* by Orazio Gentileschi; *The Last*

Brera. - Left: **Madonna and Child, Angels, Saints and Duke Federico da Montefeltro, by Piero della Francesca.** Above: detail from a fresco cycle by Donato Bramante.

Supper at Emmaus a late work by Caravaggio; *Portrait of a Knight of Malta* by Bernardo Strozzi; *the Samaritan woman at the Well* by Giovan Battista Caracciolo; *St. Jerome* by Giuseppe Ribera called Spagnoletto; *Portrait* by Luca Giordano and other works by Orazio de Ferrari.

ROOM 30. - *Self Portrait with father and grandchild* by Annibale Carracci; *Peter pays tribute* and another work by Mattia Preti; *Dance of Cupids* by Albani; *Madonna and Child* by Sassoferrato; *David with Goliath's head* by Carlo Dolci and other works by Guido Cagnacci, Ribera, Guercino.

ROOM 31. - This room and the two following ones mostly contain works by non-Italian painters. *Portrait of Amelia of Solms and Madonna with Son and St. Anthony of Padua*; both by Van Dyck; the *Last Supper* by Peter Paul Rubens; the *Samaritan* by Joachim Sandrart; *Landscape with Monks* by Alessandro Magnasco; two *Still Lives with Game* by Jan Fyt.

ROOM 32. - *St. Luke painting the Madonna*; (School of Antwerp); *Meditation of St. Francis* by El Greco; *Triptych* and *Adoration of the Magi* works by the Master of Antwerp; *St. Catherine* by the Master of the Half Figures.

ROOM 33. - *Church in a grotto, Landscape* and *Bay*, three works by Jan Brueghel the younger, *Village* by Jan Brueghel the elder; The *Nymph Syrinx and Pan* by Peter Paul Rubens and Jan Brueghel the Younger; *Portrait of Sister* by Rembrandt Van Ryn; the *Angel appears to Arauna* by Gerbrand van der Eeckhout; *Seascape* by van Goyen, the same subject by Andre van Stalbempt and other works by G.F. van Thielon.

Brera. - Madonna of the Rose Garden, by Bernardino Luini.
Right: **one of the forty-eight Tarot cards by Bonifacio Bembo.**

ROOM 34. - Italian and foreign artists: The *Madonna of Carmel* by Gian
Battista Tiepolo; *St. Paul the Hermit* by Salvator Rosa; *Portrait of Lord
Donoughmore* by Joshua Reinolds; two views of *Ruins* by Magnasco; the
Crucifixion by G. Maria Crespi; *Portrait of the singer Domenico Annibali* by
Anton Raphael Mengs; *Self-Portrait* by Giulio Carponi.

ROOM 35. - Venetian painters of the XVIIIᵗʰ Cent. *The temptation of
St. Anthony* and a sketch with *Battle* by Tiepolo; two *Views of the Grand
Canal* by Francesco Guardi; *View of Gazzada* by Bernardo Bellotto, *View
of the Grand Canal* by Canaletto; *Rebecca at the well* a masterpiece by
Piazzetta; *Portrait* by Rosalba Carriera; a *Family concert* and *the Tooth
Drawer* by Pietro Longhi.

71

Brera. - The Carrier Boy, by Giacomo Ceruti.

ROOM 36. - Italian painters of the XVIIIth Cent. *Old man praying* by Piazzetta; *Portrait of an Artist* and *Portrait of a Gentleman* by Friar Galgario; *Hannibal's Oath* by G. Battista Pittoni; *Sermon of the Baptist* by Francesco Zuccarelli and four works by Giacomo Ceruti amongst which *the Old woman* and the *Urchin* are of note.

ROOM 37. - Italian painters of the XIXth Cent. with self-portraits by Giuliano Traballesi, Martin Knoller, Giuseppe Bossi and Domenico Aspari; *Portrait of Antonio Canova* by Thomas Lawrence; *Portrait of Ugo Foscolo* by Andrea Appiani; *Portrait of Alessandro Manzoni and his second wife* by

Brera. - The Kiss, by Francesco Hayez.

Francesco Hayez by whom are also the *Forsaken Woman, the Kiss, Flowers* and the *Last moments of the Doge Martin Faliero*.

Room 38. - Italian painters of the XIX and XXth Cent. *The Bower* by Silvestro Lega; *the Red Cart* by Giovanni Fattori; *Sad Foreboding* by Cesare Cesare Tallone; *Brothers in the field* by Mosé Bianchi, the *Portrait of Count Cavour* and *Self Portrait* by Francesco Hayez.

Rooms 37-38. - These rooms are sometimes used so that the works in the deposits can be exhibited in "shifts".

New Wing. - Recently rearranged, for works painted between 1910 and 1930 by Modigliani, Boccioni, Carrà, Rosai, Sironi, De Pisis, De Chirico, etc.

One continues along via Brera as far as via Pontaccio, crosses it, then turning to the right along via Pontaccio one enters Piazza S. Marco.

ST. MARK

Tradition says this church was founded in 1254 by the Milanese
nobleman Lanfranco Settala, who then became a General of the
Augustinian order. In the 1300's it was reconstructed on a grander
scale, and in the XVth Cent. the family chapels of the nobility
along the right nave were added. In 1690 the inside was completely
transformed and decorated in Baroque style, upon a design by
Francesco Castelli. The façade, restored in 1873 is in Gothic
Lombard style and only the decorated ogival portal architrave
with *Christ between the symbols of the Evangelists and two Saints*,
remains of the older construction. In the niches of the tabernacle
above are three small statues of *Saints*. The head of the transept
still has the form of the primitive construction of the XIIIth Cent.;
the Lombard style bell-tower is of the same century.

THE INTERIOR, is completely decorated in Baroque style, in the form of a
Latin cross with three aisles divided by pillars. The chapels of the right
aisle contain interesting paintings; in the 1st, frescoes by Lomazzo with
Stories of St. Peter and St. Paul and altar piece with *Madonna and Child
with Saints*, in the 3rd, on the altar, *St. Mark* by Legnanino. In the 4th, in
the cupola, the *Descent of the Holy Ghost* perhaps by Vincenzo Campi. In
the 5th, the *Prophets* and the *Virtues* by Antonio Campi. In the right
transept various plaques and sepulchral monuments amongst which in
the middle of the central wall, the *Sarcophagus of Lanfranco Settala*
(d. 1264) a work attributed to Giovanni di Balduccio and assistants
(XIV century). On the right wall are fragments of frescoes of the
XIVth Cent.. In the chapel to the left the *Tomb* with panels in relief, is a
work attributed to Giovanni di Balduccio or Matteo da Campione, whilst
the two splendid Angels which flank the tomb on the wall facing are by
Giovanni di Balduccio. The great canvas with the *Nativity of St. Francis* is
by Legnanino. In the presbytery on the wall to the right of the great altar,
is a great canvas with the *Dispute between St. Ambrose and St. Augustine*
by Camillo Procaccini; on the left wall *Baptism of St. Augustine* , remarkable painting by Cerano (1618). In the left transept to the right: the **Chapel of
the Lamentation over the Dead Christ** with a copy of the *Deposition* by
Caravaggio above the altar, the original being in the Vatican Museum. In
the sacristy, engraved cupboards of the XVIIth Cent. and an altar piece
with the *Holy Family and St. Sirus* by Bernardino Campi (1569). Along the
left nave, on the walls: paintings by various artists, including Legnanino,
Camillo Procaccini, Palma the Younger and A. Campi.

From Piazza San Marco, via Fatebenefratelli leads to piazza
Cavour where beyond the square, behind the *monument to
Cavour*, via Palestro begins, flanked on the left by the Public
Gardens. On the right at No. 16 is the Royal Villa (Villa Reale).

Villa Reale (the Royal Villa).

VILLA REALE

One of the most beautiful neoclassical buildings in Lombardy, built by Leopoldo Pollak in 1790. The external façade is rectangular with the central part faced with rough-hewn blocks on the ground floor, while the two upper floors conform to the Ionic order. The internal façade facing the garden is, however, more beautiful: it is composed of five parts of which three are protruding and decorated with reliefs of *mythological subjects* and surrounded on the top floor by a series of statues of divinities. The bas-reliefs on the side tympanums represent the *chariot of Day* and the *chariot of Night*. The villa was originally the residence of Prince Lodovico Barbiano di Belgioioso. In 1802 the Cisalpine Republic purchased it to present it to Napoleon when he accepted the presidency of the Republic and he lived here with his wife Josephine. Eugene Beauharnais the viceroy of Italy lived here and in 1857, General Radetsky lived here until his death, on the 5th of January 1858. Finally, in 1859, the Villa passed to the Crown of Italy and then became property of the City Council. The palace now houses the Gallery of Modern Art.

MODERN ART GALLERY

Modern Art Gallery. - The Fisher-Boy, by Giovanni Gemito.

It provides a chronological display of XIXth Cent. art: from the Milanese Neoclassical movement to the Italian Romantic period, including the various Italian "Realist" schools (the Piedmontese, the Lombard, the Tuscan Macchiaioli and the Posillipo school, etc.), and the followers of the French Impressionist movement in Italy. Recent acquisitions include the Marini, the Boschi, the Fontana, the Melotti and the Vismara Collections.

Modern Art Gallery. - The Washerwomen, by Mosè Bianchi.

The **Giuseppe Vismara Collection** on the ground floor has Modigliani, Picasso, Tosi, Sironi, Morandi and other contemporary Italian and French painters.

The first floor contains the **Marino Marini Museum** with sculptures, drawings and graphic works by this artist as well as a series of portraits of cultural and artistic personalities of the XXth Cent.. One reaches the first floor by means of a staircase decorated with Neo-classical sculpture and reliefs, namely: *Hebe* by Canova, *Eve* by Baruzzi. Thence to the Picture Gallery. Among the numerous paintings on show, see the *Portrait of Alessandro Manzoni* by Hayez, paintings by Appiani and works from the "Lombard Scapigliatura" movement. See for instance works by Fontana, Medardo, Induno, Palizzi, De Nittis, Fattori, etc. Next comes **The Grassi Collection**, donated to the City by Nedda Grassi in memory of her son Gino. It is arranged in 13 rooms and includes paintings, designs, textiles, Eastern carpets and Eastern works of art. The 135 paintings constitute the essential part of the collection and the greater part belong to the XIX-XXth Cents. Thus the collection has been placed in this gallery because of its essentially modern nature. Of the XIXth Cent. Italian painters, see S. Lega (*the Haymaker; the Passing of the Holy Sacrament*) T. Signorini (*Clouds at Sunset; Oxen at Pietramala*) G. Fattori (*Great manœuvres; Trooper; Black Horse*) G. Segantini (*Dead Chamois; In the stable; Still Life*) G. de Nittis (*Femme aux pompons; Lunch at Posillipo*) A. Mancini (*In tears; Nude; In the country*) G. Boldini (*Young American Lady*), D. Ranzoni, il Piccio (*Holy Family*) O. Borrani (*Woman with candle*). Of the XXth Cent. there are G. Balla (*Child running; Villa Borghese; Car*) U. Boccioni (*Portrait of Mother; Portrait of Signora Casabianca*), G. Morandi (*Landscape; Still Life*) O. Rosai (*Landscape*) Tosi, Spadini, V. Guidi, F. Pirandello, F. Cas-

Modern Art Gallery. - Dinamism of a Human Body, by Umberto Boccioni.

orati. The French painters of the XIX-XXth Cents. include J.B. Corot (*Coup de Vent; Lady with a yellow flower*), J.F. Millet (*Return to the farm*), E. Boudin (*Washerwomen*), E. Manet (*Monsieur Armand on horseback*), P.Cezanne (*Les voleurs et l'âne*), B.Morisot (*Woman with flowers*), A. Renoir (*Walk by the sea side*), P.Gauguin (*Breton Landscape*) E. Vuillard (*Portrait of Mrs Hessel*), P. Bonnard (*Inside by lamp light*) A. Sisley (*Wind and sun*). Following the XIXth Cent. collection, comes the adjoining **Pavilion of Contemporary Art** including paintings and sculpture of the futurist period and the most recent productions. Among the painters, the works of Boccioni (very well represented here), Carrà, De Chirico, Tosi, Sironi, Campigli, De Pisis, Modigliani, Guidi, Marussig, Scipione are shown; among the sculptors: Andreotti, Martini, Manzù, Marmi, and Messina.

Almost in front of the Royal Villa is the entrance to the **Giardini Pubblici** (Public gardens), arranged in 1786 by Piermarini and transformed into an English style garden in 1862 by Giuseppe Balzaretto. Within the boundaries of the garden (which extends over an area of 17 hectares) in addition to the *Zoo*, there are the buildings which house the *Civic Museum of Natural History*.

Sant'Ambrogio, Museum of Science and Technology and Leonardo's Last Supper

On the southern side of Piazza del Duomo, to the left of Palazzo dell'Orologio, lies via degli Orefici which leads into Piazza Cordusio. On the opposite side of the square we take via Dante and immediately to the left is via Meravigli. This in turn leads into corso Magenta where to the left we find the church of the Monastero Maggiore (greater monastery).

SAN MAURIZIO (St. Mauritius) AND MONASTERO MAGGIORE

Monastero Maggiore (Church of St. Mauritius). - Interior.

It was built in 1503 by Gian Giacomo Dolcebuono and is of great artistic interest on account of the wealth of the most valued artists of the times: Bernardino Luini who worked there in the first half of the XVI century; as well as Boltraffio and Peterzano.

**Monastero Maggiore (Church of St. Mauritius). - Martyrdom of
St. Catherine, by Bernardino Luini (detail).**

THE INTERIOR is simple, it is a nave divided transversely by a wall into two
chambers; the first reserved to the worshippers; the second to the choir of
the nuns. Along the walls are two superimposed orders of pillars,
supporting the ceiling vault. A series of chapels succeed each other along
the lower order, whilst three-mullioned little loggias with graceful little
columns enhance the upper order. The whole church has its walls
completely covered in frescoes. On the internal façade are frescoes by
Simone Peterzano with the *Return of the prodigal son* and the *Eviction of
the merchants from the Temple*. The 3rd chapel on the right wall is
completely frescoed by Bernardino Luini's last work (1530), *Scenes of the
Martyrdom of St. Catherine of Alexandria*. The frescoes on the partition
wall are by Luini, whilst the *Epiphany* on the altar is by Antonio Campi
(1579). The left wall and the chapels are decorated by painters of the
XVIth Cent. including several followers of Luini. From the 3rd chapel on
the left one enters the **Nun's Choir** which has basically the same structure

as the church. Here also the partition wall, which supports the pulpit, is frescoed by Luini. The scenes which represent the *Progress to Calvary* and the *Deposition* are particularly interesting. The upper loggias contain twenty-six tondi frescoed with figures of *Saints* by Boltraffio (1510). To get to the loggias one climbs the staircase beyond the choir stalls.

To the right of the church is the entrance to the old cloister of the Monastery, now the **Civic Archeological Museum** inaugurated in 1965. The Museum contains material from the Castello Sforzesco and recently excavated archaeological finds. Continuing along corso Magenta, the vast **Palazzo Litta** rises on the right, built by Francesco M. Richini (1648) and commissioned by count Bartolomeo Arese. The great Rococo façade is by Bartolomeo Bella (1752-63). The portal is flanked by two Atlases upholding the balcony. On the upper part of the front is the coat of arms of Litta-Visconti-Arese supported by two Moors. In front of Palazzo Litta: Via Santa Agnese which leads to Piazza Sant'Ambrogio, and, beyond the basilica from which the square takes its name, lies the **Temple of Victory** erected in 1930. This austere and grandiose work is dedicated to the Milanese who lost their lives in the First World War. In the portico, in the niche in front of the entrance is the great bronze statue of St. Ambrose, by Adolf Wildt.

SANT'AMBROGIO

This is one of the oldest churches in Milan and one of the most historically interesting mediaeval buildings in Lombardy. It was begun in 379, and was a small three-aisled, transept-less church. In 386 it was consecrated by St. Ambrose who, when he died in 397, was buried beside the bodies of St. Gervase and St. Protasius inside the Church. In 739 the monastery of the Benedectine Monks was built next to the church and in the IXth Cent. the simple right bell-tower, known as the bell-tower of the monks, was erected. The apse and the presbytery were constructed in the Xth Cent., while in the XIIth Cent., the aisles, the drum, the entrance and the left bell-tower, known as the bell-tower of the Canons (in Lombard Romanesque style with pilaster strips and friezes of little hanging arches) were built. It was finished in 1889 with the completion of the three arched loggia. At the end of the XVth Cent., Cardinal Ascanio Sforza gave the task of constructing the cloisters and the portico of the rectory to Bramante. In the following centuries other changes were made, but in 1857 the Arch-Duke Maximilian of Austria ordered that the baroque additions to the church be removed. It was damaged in the August 1943 bombings, and restored by the architect Ferdinando Reggiori.

The atrium in the form of a rectangular portico, replaces the one in front of the church, built by the Archbishop Ansperto who governed the Milanese clergy from 868 to 881. It was given its present form in the first half of the XIIth Cent. The capitals of the pillars in the robust portico are sculpted with flora, symbolic animals and monstruous figures. On the walls, plaques from tombs, bas-reliefs and the sarcophagus of Archbishop Ansperto.

Sant'Ambrogio. - The porticoed atrium and the façade.

The façade, flanked on either side by the two bell-towers, is composed of two super-imposed loggias. The top one has a central arch flanked by four diminishing sized arches and below is the narthex or atrium with its three portals. The great architraves of ·the two side portals are decorated with medieval bestiary-inspired carvings. The central door lunette and architrave are carved with VIIIth and X[th] Cent. wicker patterns and monstrous creatures. The original carved wooden door with *scenes from the Life of David and Saul* date from the IVth and VIIth Cents.; the fragments are kept in the Museum of the Basilica. The two sides of the door in bronze are of the XI-XIIth Cent. To the left of the portal, marble *Sepulchre of Pier Candido Decembrio*, a humanist (d. 1477) by Tommaso Cazzaniga.

Sant'Ambrogio. - Interior.

THE INTERIOR. - This masterful and solemn church has three apsed aisles divided by pillars, with deep cross vaults and a women's gallery along the side aisles. In the central nave the capitals of the pillars are of great artistic value, to the right, *statue of Pius IX*, by Francesco Confalonieri (1880). At the third pillar to the left, three frescoes of the XIIIth Cent., representing *St. Ambrose*, the *Madonna and Child* and the *Sponsor Bonamico Taverna*. Further ahead, a column with a *Serpent* in bronze upon it, to which, legend ascribes marvellous virtues; a Byzantine work of the Xth Cent. from the East. The lovely Pulpit (damaged in 1196 by the vaults collapsing and restored in 1201) at the fifth pillar on the left: little columns supporting splendidly carved little arches are based on an ancient sarcophagus. On the left aisle side: a relief with the *Last Supper* of the XIth Cent. and also the *Angel* and *Eagle* in copper of the same epoch which decorate the front of the lectern. Under the pulpit is the *Early Christian Sarcophagus* of the IVth Cent. which tradition attributes to

Sant'Ambrogio. - Above: **the altar frontal** (detail), **by Master Volvinius.** Right: **detail of the Ciborium.**

Stilicone, the general of Theodoric and his wife Serena. The sides of the sacrophagus are decorated with reliefs: *Jesus amongst the Apostles* on the front, *Elijah on the chariot* and *Baby Jesus between the donkey and the ox* on the right, another relief of *Jesus amongst the Apostles* on the rear; the *Sacrifice of Abraham* and *Apostles* on the left. At the centre of the presbytery rises the **Ciborium**, surmounted by a lofty drum supported by four columns of porphyry with IXth Cent. capitals. The coloured stucco decoration on the canopy (XIIth Cent.) shows *Christ offering the keys to St. Peter and the book of wisdom to St. Paul* on the front; *St. Ambrose between two praying figures* to the right; *St. Ambrose between Saint Gervase and Saint Protasius*, on the side facing the apse; *Female Saint between two praying figures*, to the left. Beneath the ciborium we find the famous **Golden Altar** of 835, by the master goldsmith Volvinius, donated by the Archbishop Angilberto II (824-59). The frontal panels show *Redeemer between the symbols of the Evangelists and the Apostles* and around it *Stories from the life of Jesus*; on the back *Stories from the life of St. Ambrose*; on the sides, *Angels and Saints*. At the sides of the ciborium are two cupboards and the *Abbey Throne*. The apse, which is raised upon the crypt, has the remains of the beautiful two-row choir stalls of the XVth Cent. around it, with carved *Scenes from the life of St. Ambrose*; in the centre, marble *Chair of the Bishop* of the IXth Cent. The Byzantine style

mosaic of various epochs in the dome of the apse (which was reconstructed after the damage inflicted during the last war) shows *Christ blessing between St. Gervase and St. Protasius* in the centre and at the two sides two episodes of the vision that St. Ambrose had of the *Funeral of St. Martin at Tours*. From the sides of the presbytery one enters the **Crypt**, divided into two parts; the first, which dates back to the IXth and XIth Cent., was renovated in 1740 and has five aisles supported by red marble columns: the second, surrounded by railings, holds the *Urn of the Patron Saints* with the remains of St. Ambrose, St. Gervase and St. Protasius, by Giovanni Lomazzi from designs by Ippolito Marchetti (1897), in glass and silver. Behind, is the porphyry grave where the bodies of the three Saints were found in 1864 along with a column from Piazza Castello which indicated the place of the martyrdom of St. Gervase and St. Protasius. Along the right aisle are seven chapels. On the altar of the 2nd chapel is the *Madonna, St. Bartholomew and the Baptist*, altar piece attributed to Gaudenzio Ferrari. In the 5th chapel, which is Baroque in style, are two great XVIIIth Cent. canvases with the *Deaths of St. Benedict and St. Bernard* and below, two fragments of frescoes in the style of Luini with *Jesus in the garden* and the *Entry of Jesus into Jerusalem*. In the 6th chapel remarkable works by Lanino with the *Madonna and Child and St. John* on the altar and *Stories of St. George* on the walls. In the 7th chapel which is closed at the end by the altar with *St. Ambrose in agony*, an altar piece by Andrea Lanzani (XVIIth Cent.) to the left one enters the *ante-chapel of Saint Satirus* with frescoed vaults by Antonio de Giorgi representing the *Glory of St. Victor* (1763).

One now comes to the **Sepulchral Chamber of St. Victor in the Golden Sky** (in Ciel d'Oro), of the IVth Cent., which contained the remains of St. Victor and St. Satirus. It is a square chamber with an apse covered by a dome decorated with gleaming golden mosaics of the Vth Cent., showing an *Apotheosis of St. Victor*. On the walls are other mosaics of the same epoch representing, to the left *St. Ambrose between St. Gervase and St. Protasius* and to the right St. Felix, St. Materno and St. Naborre. In the crypt below, a sarcophagus of the Vth Cent., which served in the following centuries as a place to put relics of the martyrs. To the left of the Sepulchral Chamber, one enters the **Sacristy of the Masses** which had its vault frescoed by Tiepolo with the Apotheosis of Saint Bernard, which was however destroyed by the 1943 bombings. Two detached frescoes by Tiepolo have now been put in its place; they are the *Martyrdom of Saint Victor* and the *Shipwreck of Saint Satirus* (1737). Going back once more into the church, to the first span of the left aisle, we find the *Grape-picking Cherubs* of the V-VIth Cent. on the architrave of a door. Continuing along the aisle, in the 1st chapel, beyond the baptismal font, we find the fresco of *Christ Risen between two Angels*, by Bergognone (1491); the frescoed *Paradise* is by Isidoro Bianchi (XVIIth Cent.); A tondo with *Madonna* by Luini on the altar of the 3rd chapel. Through a door at the end of the aisle: the **Portico of the Rectory**, which was begun in 1492 by Bramante for Ludovico il Moro. It was intended to be a quadrilateral cloister, but in 1499 building was suspended when Ludovico fell from power, so only the side next to the basilica was finished. The great archways are supported by columns, four of which look like «tree trunks». Half way along the portico on the wall behind the arch, are two reliefs with the busts of *Ludovico il Moro* and *Beatrice d'Este* end of the XVth Cent. In the courtyard of the rectory is the **Oratory of St. Sigismund**, which was originally called Santa Maria Greca. It has been modified many times since the XIth Cent. and was finally restored in 1940. It is preceded by an arched portico with columns from ancient Roman buildings.

MUSEUM OF SANT'AMBROGIO

The entrance is at the end of the Rectory portico. The museum, which was founded in 1949, assembles various precious reliques of the glorious life of the basilica. The **Treasure** is placed half way down the flight of stairs. One of the most fabulous examples of the goldsmith's art, is the *Processional Cross*, of the XVth Cent. From the landing where a medallion in stucco with *the bust of St. Ambrose* of the XIIth Cent. is between two doors, one enters Room 1 known as the Tapestry Room. In Room 2 (Textiles Room) are precious textiles, known as the *Dalmatics of St. Ambrose* which include a IVth Cent. damask of Eastern origin with hunting scenes. There are also lengths of material from the sarcophagus of the Saint found in 1940 in the chapel in the transept. In Room 3, (Room of the Altar Frontals) the triptych by Bernardino Zenale representing the *Madonna and St. Ambrose and St. Jerome* (1494). There are also various altar frontals including an embroidered one of the XVth Cent. Pieces of the bombs which hit the basilica in 1943 are displayed in the corridor. Room 4 is known as the Bedstead Room because an ancient bedstead is displayed in the centre of the room which, it is believed, belonged to St. Ambrose and upon which, it seems, the Saint died. The reproduction of the ancient doors of the basilica which include several fragments of wood from the original IVth Cent. one of an exquisitely classical shape is worthy of note. Room 5, known as the Fresco Room, houses interesting works which include *Jesus amongst the doctors*, a fresco by Bergognone, and the *Madonna of the Milk*, by Luini. The showcases contain some of the 55 parchment codices which bear witness to the high artistic quality of Lombard manuscript illumination from the Xth to the XVIIIth Cents. Room 6 (Historical Room), tapestries of the XVIth Cent., drawings, prints and documents.

PUSTERLA DI SANT'AMBROGIO

After leaving the basilica of St. Ambrose, on the right hand side of Via Vittore, we find the Postern of St. Ambrose, with a double barrel-vault flanked by two towers. It was a small city-gate opened in 1171 in the old circle of the mediaeval walls, and restored in 1940. On the façade, facing towards Via De Amicis above the double barrel-vault, is a tabernacle with Gothic statues representing *St. Ambrose, St. Gervase and St. Protasius*. Inside the Postern is the *Museum of Ancient Arms* founded in 1948.

Along Via S. Vittore there is a small square on the left with the basilica of **San Vittore al Corpo**, known also as the *Basilica Porziana*; it is of Early Christian origins but was reconstructed by Vincenzo Seregni in 1560. The inside, which is richly decorated with frescoes and stuccos, contains remarkable works of art by artists of the XVIIth Cent., including Procaccini, Del Cairo, Enea Salmeggia known as «il Talpino». Nuvolone and Daniele Crespi. Left of the basilica the **Monastery of St. Victor** which contains the Leonardo da Vinci National Museum of Science and Technology.

THE LEONARDO DA VINCI NATIONAL MUSEUM OF SCIENCE AND TECHNOLOGY

The Museum, which was inaugurated on the 15th February 1953 and named after Leonardo, occupies the ancient *Monastery of the Olivetans*, near the basilica of San Vittore. It was completely reconstructed after the damage done to it during the last war and restored to its former elegant lines. The Museum tries to illustrate, in the most attractive and pleasing manner, the history of science and technology in action, the phenomena which gave birth to great inventions, discoveries, and the machines which have contributed so much to technical progress in the modern world. But in contrast with similar institutions in other countries, the Milan museum is arranged according to the three main guidelines of Leonardo's humanism: science, technology, art. The visitor thus sees ancient and modern machines side by side with experiments in physics taking place, old and new instruments in the glass cases, and famous paintings, decorations, rooms and reconstructions of environments, all of which help to make a uniquely varied and fascinating museum.

The imposing *Leonardo Gallery*, which is dominated by the severe selfportrait of the Master himself, cut into a great sheet of crystal contains the richest, most faithful and documented collection of *models* of machines, devices and projects by Leonardo in the world. In addition, the Museum has a historical-didactical Gallery of Physics, which holds the apparatus and instruments (originals or copies) of *Galileo, Newton, Volta, Pacinotti, Ferraris*, etc; show-cases where it is possible to re-perform experiments which illustrate phenomena, laws and principles. The Radio and Telecommunications section is in the *Marconi Room* and houses the most important apparatus invented and constructed by Marconi, including those once mounted aboard the yacht «*Elettra*». Note the «*Pantelegraph*» by G. Caselli (1855), the first device used in public service for the transmission of images along telegraph wires. The Typewriters section the «*Cembalo scrivano*» («Writer Clavichord») by A. Ravizza (1855). The Museum also possesses a Naval section, a Clock section with many valuable pieces; a collection of antique golden artefacts; the Transport Section which includes a great illustrated panel of the evolution of the wheel from the Ur wheel (4.000 B.C.) to the modern wheel with tyres, etc. Among the exhibits in the basement: a steam engine by Horn (around 1890); the first engines (wind-driven, hydraulic, and thermal); the history of casting, of metallurgy and of the working of metals (rolling mills, a water hammer of the XVIIth Cent. which still works perfectly). The magnificent Great Hall of the Columns once housed the library of the convent, the Refectory with magnificent XVIIIth Cent. decorations, and the Cinema. Other lesser halls frequently house congresses and meetings of great cultural interest and international importance. The library is specialized in the history of science and the teaching centre of Experimental Physics, with its classrooms and collection of instruments, the room of scientific

and technological reviews enhance and integrate the activity of the various sections ensuring valuable research assistance to the frequentors of this Museum.

Continuing along Via S. Vittore, we take a right turn along Via Bernardino Zenale which leads once more to Corso Magenta. Immediately ahead lies Piazza Santa Maria delle Grazie, with the church from which it gets its name.

SANTA MARIA DELLE GRAZIE

Santa Maria delle Grazie. - The façade.

Santa Maria delle Grazie is the most evocative church of Milan. It is a blend of the Gothic and Renaissance style by Guiniforte Solari and Donato Bramante. It is built upon the site of a former chapel with a fresco of the Madonna, known as Madonna delle Grazie. The construction of the church, designed by Guiniforte Solari, commissioned by the Domenicans, was started in 1466

Santa Maria delle Grazie. - Overall view.

(when the adjoining Monastery was practically finished) and completed in 1490. Shortly after, however, Ludovico il Moro, who was very fond of this church, decided to modify and enlarge it with the intention of having a Memorial to himself and his wife Beatrice d'Este added to the church as well. Once the presbytery and the apse were demolished, Bramante began constructing the magnificent apse formed by a great tri-apsidal cube with a marvellous decoration of tondi in the bands of the base, with Sforza coats of arms and medallions in marble and male and female Saints in the upper parts (the latter are attributed to Amadeo). Within the apse rises the polygonal drum with mullioned windows and a graceful gallery upholding the dome. In 1497 Beatrice d'Este was buried in this church but, due to the political events of the time, Ludovico il Moro could not be buried beside her and the statues by Solari for the tombs of Ludovico il Moro and his wife, are now in the Charterhouse of Pavia. From 1558 to 1782 the Tribunal of the Inquisition had its headquarters in the monastery. In 1934-37 the whole building was consolidated and restored under the direction of the architect Piero Portaluppi, thanks to the generosity of the senator Ettore Conti, who then also financed the renovations (in 1947), after the serious damage done to the Refectory of the Monastery and the main body of the

Santa Maria delle Grazie. - The apse.

Church during the 1943 bombings. The façade, which is wide and low, is in traditional Lombard style. It is divided by pilaster strips and has four gothic windows in the lower part and oculi in the upper part. The marble porch in the form of a shrine, which is supported by columns and pillars, is by Bramante. In the lunette of the deep porch arch, is a fresco by Michelangelo Bellotti (1729). Along the right side of the church are paired ogival windows with round oculi set between the points of each pair.

INTERIOR. - The church has three aisles divided by wide ogival arches supported by columns and with cross vaults with various frescoed decorations. Along the side aisles-square chapels. Above the arches of the nave, in the lunettes, are tondi with half figures of *Dominican Saints* by Bernardino Butinone and full figures of *Domenican Saints* on the pillars (XVth Cent.) also by Butinone. In the 1st chapel of the right aisle, on the left wall, the *Tombs of the Della Torre family*, with three bas-reliefs on the front

Santa Maria delle Grazie. - Interior.

of the sarcophagus showing the *Annunciation*, the *Adoration of the Shepherds* and the *Epiphany*, by Francesco Cazzaniga (1483). Above the altar is a beautiful fresco removed from its original place, of the *Madonna adoring the Child* by an unknown Lombard artist of the XVth Cent. 2nd chapel: four XVIth Cent. centaphs. The 4th chapel is decorated with frescoes by Gaudenzio Ferrari (1542) with *History of the Passion and Angels*. In the 5th chapel the walls are decorated with stucco Angel festoon bearers (XVIth Cent.). The chapel vault and the upper sections of the walls are decorated with frescoes by Giovanni De' Mio. The 6th chapel has a *Madonna and Saints*, by Coriolano Malagnazzo (XVIth Cent.) and frescoes on the walls by the Fiammenghini brothers. The 7th chapel frescoes and stuccoes on the vault by Ottavio Semini and *the Baptist worshipped by Count Vimercati*, by Marco d'Oggiono. We now come to the apse by Bramante with four powerful arches upholding the dome supported by a drum surrounded by a loggia crowned by a decorative frieze, the whole being a perfect Renaissance work of art. The presbytery is square in form and opens into a great niche. The vault is umbrella shaped, with round oculi in the lunettes at its base. On the walls are graffiti of *Dominican Saints*. In the pendentives of the arches and of the lunettes, are medallions with busts of the *Evangelists* and the *Doctors* attributed to Amadeo. The beautiful wooden choir has two rows of inlaid stalls with figures of Saints and floral motifs (1470-1510). Between the presbytery and the left aisle is the **Chapel of the Madonna delle Grazie** which was the oratory of the first church constructed here, which was then incorporated in the subsequent reconstruction and later enlarged and decorated with stuccos and paintings, unfortunately mostly destroyed by the 1943 bombings. On the front of the span facing the nave is a great XVIIth Cent. composition in stucco showing the *Madonna delle Grazie*, a much venerated image during the plagues of 1576 and 1630. The 4th chapel of the left aisle (chapel of senator Conti), closed by a bronze XVIIth Cent. railing, has a triptych on the altar with the *Madonna and Saints* by Niccolò da Cremona. In the 2nd chapel, are the *Funeral Stelae of Cardinal Arcimboldi* with sculptures attributed to Bambaia and the *Funeral plaques of Cardinal Branda Castiglioni* (d. 1495). In the 1st chapel, the remains of frescoes by Montorfano, and a modern bas-relief by Arrigo Minerbi on the altar. Returning to the apse, through a door to the left, we enter the **Small Cloister** by Bramante which Ludovico il Moro had built. It is a small court with a harmonious porticoed walk all the way around; the arches are supported by graceful tapered columns with exquisitely worked capitals. In the lunette of the door which leads to the church, flanking a small shrine, is a fresco with *St. Peter* and *St. Catherine*, by Bramantino who also painted the one in the lunette above the portal on the opposite side of the portico with *Madonna and Child with Saints*. The door leads into the **Old Sacristy**, also by Bramante with two-storey cupboards all round the walls, inlaid and painted with *Stories from the Old and New Testaments* (1497-1503). On the internal face of the side pillars of the apse are bas-reliefs with portraits of *Ludovico il Moro* and his son *Maximilian*.

LAST SUPPER (LEONARDO DA VINCI)

To the right of the church is the ex-monastery of the Dominicans in the Refectory of which Ludovico il Moro ordered Leonardo to paint the Last Supper (1495-98), one of the world's greatest painted masterpieces. The painting occupies the wall at the end; in the three top lunettes, connected to the decorations of the vault (which was destroyed in 1943) are the coats of arms of the Sforzas and the Estes within garlands, as a homage to the Duke Ludovico il Moro and Beatrice d'Este. Some people maintain that the scene by Leonardo of the twelve Apostles seated together with their Master at the Supper table, portrays them when Jesus announced that one of them would betray him, or, as other say, at the moment of the Consecration. The Disciples' emotion transpires from their gestures, movements and faces and contrasts with the

Santa Maria delle Grazie. - View from the cloister. Overleaf: **the Last Supper, by Leonardo da Vinci, in the refectory.**

apparent immobility of Christ who dominates the centre of a rigorously symmetrical composition in perfect perspective. The whole scene is bathed in a diffuse, gentle light coming partly from three windows at the far end of the room and partly from the light at the front which seems to come from the actual window in the real room. The painting was miraculously untouched by the bombings of August 1943 which damaged the nearby cloisters and parts of the church. Unfortunately the fresco is rather spoilt. From 1517 it has steadily deteriorated, mainly because of the new technique experimented by Leonardo. At the time of Napoleon the refectory was used as a stable and in 1801 was flooded by water. After having escaped from the bombings of 1943, in 1953 it was given a cleaning and consolidation; it has been further restored recently. The great fresco, at the other end of the hall, of the *Crucifixion* is by Donato di Montorfano (1499).

From the south west corner of Piazza del Duomo one takes via Orefici where, at a certain point, one turns to the left along Via Cesare Cantù which leads into the square which contains **Palazzo dell'Ambrosiana**, built by Lelio Buzzi (1609) urged on by Cardinal Federico Borromeo.

PINACOTECA AMBROSIANA

The Ambrosian Art Gallery founded in 1618 by Cardinal Federico Borromeo, is renowned for the great value of the works of art displayed, mostly of the XVth, XVIth and XVIIth Cents.

From the entrance one climbs the great staircase where there are two plaster casts of the *Pietà* by Michelangelo from S. Peter's in the Vatican and the *Lacoon*, the original of which is to be found in the Vatican Museums. At the top of the staircase on the walls are two great canvases with *Alpine Landscapes* by the Flemish painter Brill. Access to the art gallery on the left. In the following description of the rooms, only the most renowned works are mentioned.

ROOM 1. - *Madonna and Child with Angels*, beautiful painting by Sandro Botticelli; *Nativity* by Ghirlandaio; two works by Bergognone: *The Madonna and Child, Angels, Saints, and the patron* from the first period (around 1490), and *St. Elizabeth and St. Francis; Pietà* by Lippo Vanni; *Madonna and the patron* by Pinturicchio. In addition, works by Bartolomeo Vivarini, Marco Basaiti, Butinone and others.

ROOM 2. - Longobard sculpture from the VIIIth to the XIth Cent.

ROOM 3. - The sculpted fragments from Bambaia's *tomb of Gaston de Foix* are particularly interesting. The frescoes on the right wall are by Lombard painters from the end of the XVth Cent.

Santa Maria delle Grazie (Refectory). - **Last Supper** (detail), **by Leonardo da Vinci.**

Pinacoteca Ambrosiana (Ambrosian Art Gallery). - Enthroned Madonna and Child with Saints and Patron, by Bergognone.

ROOM 4. - German and Flemish painters, including an *Adoration of the Magi* by Joos Van Cleve.

ROOM 5. - A number of paintings as well as Cardinal Federico Borromeo's silver *Holy water Stoup* with miniatures by Jan Breughel the Younger.

ROOM 6. - The works of Flemish and German artists continue, with various miniatures by Jan Breughel the Younger, including the famous *Water* and *Fire* which are part of the *Four Elements* quartet (*Earth* and *Air* are in Paris).

ROOM 7. - Bernardino Luini's famous *St. John* together with his *Christ raising his hand in blessing* and his *Madonna suckling the Child*. Besides,

Pinacoteca Ambrosiana. - Basket of Fruit, by Caravaggio.

Adoration of the Child, by the young Bramantino; *Madonna and Child*, by Giampietrino; *St. Jerome* by Andrea Solari.

ROOM 8. - Two famous portraits by Leonardo are displayed here: the *Musician* (perhaps a portrait of Franchino Gaffurio) and *Beatrice d'Este* (some people maintain that this is a portrait of the Duchess of Milan by Ambrogio de Predis). The *Holy Family* by Bernardino Luini, which is derived from a cartoon by Leonardo. The triptych with the *Madonna of Saint Michael* is by Bramantino at the height of his career. In addition, *Nativity* by Giampietrino and *Madonna and Child*, and *Sts. John the Baptist and John the Evangelist*, a triptych by Marco d'Oggiono.

ROOM 9. - *Judith* by Parmigianino; *Madonna and Child and St. John as a boy* by Giuliano Bugiardini; *Holy Family*, by Sodoma.

ROOM 10. - On the wall at the end is a great cartoon by Raphael for the *School of Athens*, the only one that remains, by the great artist, of the ones he prepared for his Rooms of the Vatican. We also find here the cartoon by Giulio Romano for the *Battle of Constantine*, a fresco which is in the "Room of Constantine" also in the Vatican. In addition, various cartoons by Pellegrino Tibaldi for the stained glass windows of the Cathedral and one by Giuseppe Bossi with an *Allegorical figure*. The altar piece of the *Annunciation* is by Gerolamo Mazzola.

Pinacoteca Ambrosiana. - The School of Athens, detail of the cartoon drawn by Raphael for the Vatican fresco.

ROOM 11. - This room contains works by Baroque artists. The most important are Gian Battista Tiepolo's sketch of the *Presentation at the Temple* and the *Bishop Saint*; young Caravaggio's famous *Basket of Fruit* and the well-known *Nativity* by Barocci. In addition, *Magdalen* by Guido Reni, *Bacchanal* by Magnasco, *Portrait* by Fra' Galgario, *Allegory* by Salvator Rosa, and other works by G. Cesare Procaccini, Palma the Younger, Cesare Ligari, Morazzone (to whom the *Adoration of the Magi* is attributed) and others.

ROOM 12. - Dedicated to artists of the neo-classical period. The *model of the Triumphal Arch* in gilded bronze, placed in the middle of the room, is by Luigi Cagnola. The two marble busts are the self-portraits of Canova and Thorvaldsen. Among the various paintings there is a series of portraits by Andrea Appiani, including those of *Napoleon* and of *Signora Rua*. In the showcase, Empire golden artefacts.

ROOM 13. - Dedicated to Venetian painters: Titian's *Deposition*, *Ecce Homo*, *Epiphany* (which he painted with his assistants), *Portrait of warrior* (unfinished), and the *Magdalen*. *The Adoration of the Magi* by Schiavone; *Portrait of a man on horseback* by G. Battista Moroni; *St. Peter the Martyr* by Moretto; *Jesus at Calvary* by Cariani.

Returning to the entrance, ROOM 14 is on the right and is normally used for conferences. XVIIth Cent. Lombard mannerist painters are hung here, including *Madonna with St. Francis and Charles*, an early painting by Davide Crespi; *St. Ambrose*, by Cerano; *Dispute of Jesus at the Temple*, by Morazzone, and other works by Panfilo and Figino.

From the entrance access also into the **Ambrosian Library**. This is the famous institution which was founded and opened to the public in 1609 by Cardinal Federico Borromeo, archbishop of Milan, of whom Manzoni also

Pinacoteca Ambrosiana. - Portrait of a Musician, by Leonardo da Vinci.

wrote in the "Betrothed". He endowed the library with manuscript codices and books from all the countries of Europe and Asia. It has grown over the centuries and now has **35.000 manuscripts**, **3.000 incunabula** and **700.000** books and periodicals. It has had many illustrious librarians amongst whom Muratori, Cardinal Mai and Achille Ratti who later became Pope Pius XI. Amongst the most famous manuscripts we note *Ilias Picta* a Graeco-Bizantine manuscript of the Vth-VIth Cent., illuminated with Classical illustrations; the *Virgil* which belonged to Petrarch (with his hand-written notes) illuminated by Simone Martini XIVth Cent.; the palimpsests of Cicero and Plato; the 1353 *Divine Comedy*; the *Irish Codex*; the *Provençal Codex*, the Gothic *Ulfilas* and the famous **Atlantic Codex** (hand-written by Leonardo da Vinci himself). There are numerous *Papyri, Hour Books*, parchments and *illuminated codices* and also great Master drawings. In addition one finds here the *Charles Borromeo* and his cousin *Cardinal Federico*, the archives and the Beccaria collection.

SANT'EUSTORGIO

St. Eustorgius. - Overall view.

St. Eustorgius is one of the most remarkable Mediaeval monuments in Milan. We do not know when the church was first started and only a few stones of the tiny basilica, which rose in the IVth Cent. upon the burial place of archbishop St. Eustorgius, are left. It was then incorporated in the larger church constructed towards the end of the XIth Cent. in Romanesque-Cluniac style. Barbarossa almost destroyed the whole thing and in 1164 had the presumed relics of the Three Kings (Magi), which tradition has, were given to St. Eustorgius by Emperor Constantine, transported to Cologne. In the XIIth Cent. the reconstruction in Ro-

St. Eustorgius. - Exterior of Portinari chapel and belltower.

manesque style was begun and from this period the beautiful apse has remained, with its external arches on the upper register. The most important transformations took place in 1220 when the Dominicans moved in and then, after the death of St. Peter Martyr in 1252, the building of the church commenced, lasting several centuries. The family chapels along the right side jut out: first come the XVth Cent. ones, then the cusped XIVth Cent. ones with arches at the lower level and ogival or mullioned windows. The XIIIth Cent. transept chapels also protude from the main body of the Church. After the Romanesque apse comes the cusped

St. Eustorgius. - Interior.

belltower, 75 metres high and built in the years 1279-1309. It is a typical Lombard belltower with mullioned openings in the bell-chamber. Next, after a XVth Cent. chapel comes the graceful exterior of the famous *Portinari Chapel*, of the same period, composed of a square body and polygonal drum. The façade (renovated in 1863-65) has three portals and five windows, the two side ones and the central one being mullioned. The decorated frieze along the top of the façade and the little brick arches are part of the original façade. On the left corner, is a stone porched shrine on a column, built in 1579 to replace the original wooden one from which St. Peter Martyr preached.

THE INTERIOR. - is 70 metres long and 24 metres wide, it has three aisles divided into eight spans by large pillars with the typical XIth to XIIIth Cent. type capitals carved with little monstrous figures and twining tendrils. The fourth pillar to the left is interesting, it shows the *Urn of the Magi being carried in procession*. In the right aisle after the third chapel, the spans are incorporated into the chapels that follow. The first chapel of the *Brivios* was constructed in 1484 and restored in the XIXth Cent.. The tryptych which has been split up, with *Madonna and Saints* is by Bergognone. On

St. Eustorgius. - The Portinari chapel dome.

the left wall the *Funeral Monument to Giovanni Stefano Brivio* (died 1484) by Francesco Cazzaniga and his brother Tommaso and Benedetto Briosco (1486). The 2nd, the *Torelli Chapel*, was constructed in 1424. The statue of *St. Dominic* on the altar is by Carlo Rainoldi (1736) and the relief on the altar-front is also by him. On the left wall, *Sepulchre of Pietro Torelli* (died 1412), admirably sculpted by a Campione master-carver. The frescoes on the walls are by Giovanni Mauro Fiammenghino. The 3rd chapel was rebuilt in the Baroque style in the XVIIIth Cent. by Francesco Croce, and the restored *Sarcophagus of Protaso Caimi*, by Bonino da Campione (around 1360) has been placed against the left wall. Above *St. Ambrose on horseback* by Ambrogio Figino. On the right wall, an XVIIIth Cent. altarpiece with the *Madonna and Dominican Saints*. The 4th chapel, of the *Viscontis*, contains the *Mausoleum of Stefano Visconti* (died 1327) and his wife *Valentina Doria* (died 1359) by Giovanni di Balduccio da Pisa and by Bonino da Campione who remade the Sarcophagus of Visconti's wife after her death. On the wall, above the mausoleum is the masterpiece of a Lombard Master of the XIVth Cent., *Saint George and the Princess*. The frescoes to be found on the vault and on the left wall are also by Lombard masters of the XIVth Cent. Beneath the frescoes, a lovely *Crucifix* upon wood, by an Emilian Master of the beginning of the XIVth Cent. In the 5th chapel on the altar, *Madonna and Child with Saints*, attributed to Cerano.

In the 6th chapel, which belonged to the cadet branch of the Visconti family, to the right, *Tomb of Gaspare Visconti* (died 1434) probably by a Rhineland master from the beginning of the XVth Cent.. To the left, *Tomb of Umberto Visconti*, with reliefs on the sarcophagus and a *Pietà* (above) by Bonino da Campione. Underneath, inscription from the tomb with the reclining figure of *Agnese Besozzi* the second wife of Gaspare Visconti, by Iacopino da Tradate (1420). In the 7th chapel, of the *Torriani Family*, fairly recently restored, XVth Cent. frescoes in the vault. From the right transept, where, above two arches to the left there is a fresco of *the Adoration of the Magi* attributed to Luini, one enters the *Chapel of the Magi* which contains the great Roman sarcophagus, in which the presumed relics of the three Magi were kept until 1164, when they were taken to Cologne. Above the altar is a tri-part reredos showing episodes from the *Stories of the Three Kings*, by a XIVth Cent. Po-Valley Master. In the presbytery, on the main altar is a great marble reredos divided into panels, with *Stories of the Passion*, a masterpiece by various artists of successive periods starting from the beginning of the XIVth Cent. Below the altar is an urn containing the remains of St. Eustorgius, St. Magnus and St. Honoratus, Milanese bishops. Behind the altar, *Angels and Saints*, fresco by Gaudenzio Ferrari. From the presbytery one enters the pseudo-crypt, erected in 1537 for which the XVth Cent. columns from the adjoining Dominican cloister were used. The frescoes on the walls, representing *Procession of Saints* and the *Legend of the Seven Sleepers* are by Lombard painters of the XVIth Cent. To the right we enter a chapel, built in 1575, while a wide cross-vaulted corridor runs-off left where a XIIIth Cent. multi-coloured stone statue of *St. Eugene* stands. The door to the left leads into the Sacristy, with beautiful XVIIth Cent. carved cupboards. The corridor leads to a room which serves as a vestibule to the Portinari chapel opposite, and to the two side chapels. The right XIVth Cent. Gothic cross-vaulted one, has a fresco on the wall by a XVth Cent. Lombard master showing *Jesus, St. Dominic and a votary* as well as *St. Francis* by Chignoli. In the chapel to the left are the remains of frescoes by Daniele Crespi and *Madonna and Child* by a painter of the XVth Cent.. Through the archway flanked by two bronze candelabra one enters the **Portinari Chapel** dedicated to St. Peter Martyr, a Tuscan style early Renaissance architectural jewel.

The noble Florentine *Pigello Portinari* had it built in 1462 while he was the procurator of the Medici Bank and the chapel was intended to shelter the remains of St. Peter Martyr and as a tomb for himself. It has not been ascertained who the builder was, but it is generally attributed to the Florentine architect Michelozzo Michelozzi, whom Portinari had given the task of decorating the Milanese branch of the Medici bank that very year. The interior is square surmounted by a circular dome and a niche-like chamber for the altar. A procession of *Festoonbearing Angels* in coloured stucco by a Lombard decorator upon designs by a Tuscan master runs around the cylindrical drum, against a background of elegant little arches. The cycle of frescoes with the *Annunciation*, the *Assumption* and *Episodes from the Life of St. Peter Martyr* which decorate the chapel, is a masterpiece of Vincenzo Foppa, a great Lombard artist of the XVth Cent., who painted it in 1468. The celebrated *Tomb of St. Peter Martyr* sculpted by Giovanni di Balduccio da Pisa between 1336 and 1339 is in the centre of the chapel. It contains the remains of the Saint. The sarcophagus in white marble decorated with bas-reliefs representing episodes in the life of the Saint, is supported by eight columns flanked by eight statues symbolizing the Virtues. The sarcophagus with a cover in the form of a truncated pyramid is surmounted by a three-cusped shrine containing the statues of the *Madonna and Child* between *St. Dominic* and *St. Peter Martyr*. Inside the

St. Eustorgius. - (The Portinari chapel), the tomb of St. Peter the Martyr, by Giovanni di Balduccio da Pisa.

small chapel, to the left of the altar-chamber the skull of the Saint is kept in a precious silver tabernacle. Returning to the presbytery one turns down the left aisle, the chapels of which contain XIIIth Cent. detached frescoes. In the 7th chapel a *Deposition* by Camillo Procaccini; in the 5th chapel, *monument of G.P. Varisio* of the XVth Cent. and *Slab from the tomb of the Bishop Federico Maggi* (died 1333) by a Campione artist.

SAN LORENZO MAGGIORE

San Lorenzo Maggiore. - Rear view of the basilica.

Sixteen *Fluted Columns* from a IInd or IIIrd Cent. Roman building were moved here in the IVth Cent. to form the pronaos of the great porticoed courtyard in front of the basilica. They are the most significant remains of Roman and Early Christian Mediolanum. The bronze statue of the *Emperor Constantine* (a copy of the one in the Lateran stands in the centre of the courtyard. In 313 Constantine issued the famous edict granting the Christians religious freedom, in Milan. The basilica was constructed towards the middle of the IVth Cent., as the Arian cathedral of Milan and became a Catholic church in the Vth Cent. Architecturally, the structure is an example of the old, majestic, central plan construction, typical of western Christianity. It suffered devastating fires in the XIth and XIIth Cents.; it was restored in the Romanesque period and finally when part of the structure collapsed in the XVIth Cent., St. Charles Borromeo had it substantially restored by Martino Bassi who added the cupola (1574). He however maintained the original, centrally oriented plan with its four corner turrets. The modern porticoed façade is by Cesare Nava (1894).

S. Lorenzo Maggiore. - The façade.

THE INTERIOR, solemn and majestic thanks to the great dome and the four deep-set exedrae, has a wide walk-way surmounted by women's galleries which reminds one of San Vitale in Ravenna. On the right, traces of mosaics of the XIV th Cent. representing the *Crucifixion and figures of Saints*. Through a *Roman door* of the 1st century A.D. one enters the chapel of *St. Aquilinus* which was built at the same time as the main church, preserving the IV th Cent. architecture. It is octagonal with niches,

San Lorenzo Maggiore. - The chapel of St. Aquilinus.

women's galleries and covered by a cupola. In the two end-niches Roman
Christian mosaics of the IVth Cent. of *Jesus between the Apostles* and a
fragmentary scene of *Elijah in his fiery chariot*. In the other niches are
Early Christian sarcophagi, including the Vth Cent. one on the right, which
according to tradition held the remains of Gallia Placidia. The frescoed
Pietà in the lunette of the archway at the entrance is attributed to
Bergognone. A staircase leads to the *Women's Galleries* with IVth Cent.
frescoes decorating it. From the chapel at the bottom, with the *Silver Tomb*
containing the body of St. Aquilinus, one descends into the vast crypt
containing stone blocks from a Roman building of the II Cent. Returning
to the church, on the wall, near the entrance to the chapel is an admirable
XIIIth Cent. fresco of the *Deposition from the Cross*. Continuing, we pass
under the tower with frescoes on the pillar and to the right *The Tomb of the
Robiani* of the XVth Cent. Further ahead lies the **Cittadini Chapel** of
Romanesque origins with XVth Cent. Gothic additions, in which there are
the remains of IVth Cent. frescoes. Continuing along as far as the main
altar we find the **Chapel of St. Hippolytus**. The interior is in the form of a
Greek cross and the columns at the corners come from a building of the
Imperial epoch. Under the tower that follows, the *sepulchre of Giovanni del
Conte*, by Marco d'Agreste and Vincenzo Seregni. Next comes the **Chapel
of St. Sixtus** preceeded by a small atrium. It was constructed in the
Vth Cent. and has an octagonal interior with XVIIth Cent. frescoes on the
vault by Storer. Further on is an old fresco which is a reproduction of the
Last Supper by Leonardo.

S. Maria della Passione. - The Baroque façade.

SANTA MARIA DELLA PASSIONE

The construction of this vast building was begun towards the end of the XVth Cent. by Giovanni Battagio who gave it the form of a Greek cross. The great cupola was completed in 1530 and towards the end of the XVIth Cent., Martino Bassi who had the task of enlarging it, prolonged the foot of the cross transforming it into a Latin one. The Baroque façade which is adorned with statues and reliefs is by Giuseppe Rusnati who completed it in 1729.

THE INTERIOR, in the form of a Latin cross, has a main arm with three aisles divided by pillars. Busts of *Saints and Members of the Lateran Order* painted on canvas by Daniele Crespi are hung at the base of the pillars. Admirable XVIth and XVIIth Cent. paintings in the side and transept chapels. In the 3rd chapel to the right, the *Offertory* by Daniele Crespi and the *Crowning with thorns* by Cerano. In the 5th chapel the XVIth Cent. fresco, donated by the founder Archbishop Daniele Birago, showing the *Madonna of the Passion*, which gave the church its name. In the 6th chapel *Madonna of Caravaggio* by Bramantino. At the base of the half columns beneath the vast octagon of the cupola, paintings by Daniele Crespi with *Scenes of the Passion*. In the chapel of the right transept, on the altar, *Deposition* by Bernardino Luini (1516); on the right wall *Jesus among the*

S. Maria della Passione. - The organ loft and the main altar.

Apostles a fragment of a poliptych perhaps by Bergognone; the frescoes of the apse with the *Madonna at the sepulchre* and "*Noli me tangere*" and those on the vault with the *Prophets* and *Evangelical Scenes* are by Antonio Campi. Under the organ in the niche to the right of the presbytery, *Funeral Monument of the Archbishop Daniele Birago*, founder of the church by Andrea Fusina (1495). In the sacristy, on the walls and in the higher lunettes, frescoes by Bergognone. In the apse, a carved wooden XVIth Cent. choir stall, two canvases by Francesco Lanfranco with *Resurrection* and *Ascension* and frescoes by Nuvolone in the half-vault showing the *Coronation of Mary* and *Evangelists and Sibylls* on the ceiling-vault. On the altar of the chapel in the left transept *Last Supper*, by Gaudenzio Ferrari (1543); on the wall *Crucifixion* by Giulio Campi. In the chapel along the left aisle, various interesting paintings, including Daniele Crespi's *St. Charles fasting* in the I[st] chapel.

San Satiro. - View of the church from the apse.

SAN SATIRO

The church was founded by Bishop Ansperto in 876. It was a small church built on a piece of ground belonging to his family. The reconstruction was begun in 1478 by Bramante who added the octagonal sacristy which to-day is the baptistery. The façade which was begun by Amadeo in 1486 upon a design by Bramante, was left unfinished and was given its modern appearance its by Giuseppe Vandoni in 1871. The reliefs prepared by Amadeo, which were intended to be placed in the tondi, are now kept in the Castello Sforzesco. The exterior of the apse is interesting, with its two side-portals and the cylindrical drum topped by an elegant lantern. To the right is the picturesque exterior of the XVth Cent. *Chapel of the Pietà* cylindrical in form with niches and an octagonal drum. The XIth Cent. belltower rises beside it: a veritable prototype of Lombard architecture.

THE INTERIOR, notwithstanding the modest proportions of the church, is nobly spacious and admirably proportioned. It has three aisles, divided by pillars with a transept. The splendid coffered dome rises above the point at which the vaults of the transept and main nave meet. Behind the main altar, a series of terracotta pilasters designed by Bramante provides an illusorily deep apse. At the end of the left arm of the transept, one enters the **Chapel of the Pietà**, which has maintained the original IXth Cent. Ansperto structure. Above the altar in the niche is a *Deposition* composed of 14 figures in coloured terracotta, by Agostino De Fondutis (1483). To the right of the entrance, *Saints* and *Madonna and Child*: X[th] Cent. Byzantine style frescoes. From the right aisle, one enters the **Sacristy** or **Baptistery**, an elegant creation by Bramante, octagonal in form with two rows of loggias and a dome. The *Putti, Angels* and the *Male Busts* which form the freize along the top, are in coloured terracotta by Agostino de Fondutis upon a model by Bramante.

SANTA MARIA NEAR SAN CELSO

The sanctuary is preceeded by a large elegant atrium with porticos (1513) flanked by the remains of the old church of St. Celsus built in the Xth Cent., with a XIIIth Cent. Romanesque belltower. The construction of the church of St. Mary was begun in 1493 by the architect Gian Giacomo Dolcebuono after which Cristofaro Solari and Giovanni Antonio Amadeo took over and finished in 1505. In 1513 Cesariano was asked to enlarge the church, but he only completed the porticoed atrium, while the interior was modified by Cristoforo Lombardo and finished by Vincenzo Seregni in 1563. The façade, begun in 1565 by Galeazzo Alessi and finished by Martino Bassi, who succeeded him, is divided into four orders and surmounted by a tympanum. The statues of *Adam and Eve* in the shrines of the lower order, flanking, the sides of the three portals, the *Angel*, the *Virgin of the Annunciation* and the relief above the central portal are by Stoldo Lorenzi, whilst the *Sybil* on the portal, the four *Prophets* in the side niches, the Angels with the *Madonna* (a copy) in the tympanum and the basreliefs are by Annibale Fontana. The polygonal drum with the series of mullioned windows is by Dolcebuono.

THE INTERIOR is a Latin cross with three aisles supported by pillars, a great barrel vault with dome and presbytery surrounded by a walk-way. Besides the beautiful XVIth Cent. decorations (note the lovely gilded coffered vaults) the church boasts many beautiful works of art. The niches at the bottom of the columns which support the cupola in the central nave contain, to the left a statue of the *Baptist* and to the right a statue of *Elijah*,

Santa Maria near San Celso. - The façade.

both by Stoldo Lorenzi. Against the following column, a statue of *St. John the Evangelist* by Annibale Fontana; below: an epigraph dedicated to the artist buried here. *Altar of the Madonna* by Martino Bassi against the opposite column with a statue of the *Assumption* by Fontana (1586), who also made the bronze candelabrum left of the main altar. In the 4th Chapel of the right aisle: *Martyrdom of St. Nazaire and St. Celsus,* by Cesare Procaccini (1607). On the altar of the right transept, *Holy Family and St. Jerome* by Paris Bordone. The arches along the walk way contain a series of canvases, amongst which, in the fourth arch, *Baptism of Jesus* by Gaudenzio Ferrari and in the seventh *Conversion* of *St. Paul* by Moretto da Brescia. The altar at the end of the left transept is composed of a sarcophagus of the IVth Cent., containing the body of St. Celsus, placed there by St. Ambrose. In the 3rd chapel of the left aisle, *Martyrdom of St. Catherine* by Cerano (1603), in the 1st chapel *Madonna adoring the Child* by Bergognone. Above the portal, statue of the *Madonna* by Annibale

117

Fontana, which was originally on the façade, and has now been substituted by a copy. The Treasure Sacristy, used to contain the so-called Chiaravalle *Processional Cross* in red jasper, gold and gems, which is now elsewhere, and an *anfora* of gilded silver, attributed to Benvenuto Cellini, together with chalices, relics, monstrances etc.

SAN CARLO AL CORSO

San Carlo al Corso. - The façade.

The church dedicated to St. Charles was planned by Carlo Amati between 1832 and 1847, upon the site of the pre-existing church of Santa Maria dei Servi. It has a Corinthian pronaos flanked by porticos. Architecturally it is a central plan construction covered by a dome, supported by Corinthian columns, erected without scaffolding by Felice Pizzagalli; niche-like chapels are built between the Corinthian columns. In the third chapel to the right *Deposition*, by Pompeo Marchesi ordered by Ferdinand and Francis I[st] of Austria; in the third chapel to the left *St. Charles giving Holy Communion to St. Luigi Gonzaga* by Marchesi.

The portico of the Lazzaretto.

THE LAZZARETTO

Only a part of the portico in Via San Gregorio remains to-day of the old Lazzaretto mentioned by Manzoni, after its demolition in 1882. The remains give some idea of the great building which covered a squarish area marked-off by Via San Gregorio, Via Lazzaretto, Viale Vittorio Veneto and Corso Buenos Aires as they are today. It was planned by the "Captains and defenders of the city of Milan" as a hospital to isolate and heal the plague-ridden inhabitants at the time of the Ambrosian Republic (1447). The construction of the building under the direction of Lazzaro Palazzi, went on until 1513. Three sides of the portico lead into 228 little cells; in the centre rose a small church which was rebuilt by order of Bishop Charles Borromeo after the plague of 1576, and was renamed San Carlo al Lazzaretto (in Via Lecco).

San Nazaro Maggiore. - Overall view.

SAN NAZARO MAGGIORE

The church was founded in the IVth Cent. by St. Ambrose who had the remains of St. Nazarus transferred there. The original outside walls of the church have survived, whilst the rest was re-built in the XIth Cent. The XIth Cent. apse remains but most of the rest was restructured during one of the many successive alterations.

THE INTERIOR of the church is preceeded by the *Funeral Chapel of the Trivulzio Family*, octagonal in form, with a cupola constructed in 1512 by Bramantino, commissioned by Marshall Gian Giacomo Trivulzio. In the niches are eight tombs with reclining statues of the Trivulzios. The one in front of the entrance is the *sarcophagus of Gian Giacomo Trivulzio*, sculpted by Francesco Brioso, and bears the famous Latin inscription "Qui numquam quievit quiescit: tace" (he who never found peace now rests: silence). The interior of the church is in the form of a Greek cross with a great dome and a deep apse. The XVth Cent. fresco on the altar on the left wall shows *Madonna and Child and St. Matronianus* and the XIIIth Cent. frescoed *Christ who appears to Mary Magdalen* is at the same altar. In the right transept, in the niche, *Last Supper* a copy by Lanino of the work by Gaudenzio Ferrari. Opposite the *Altar of St. Matronianus* and on the wall, a bas-relief with a *Crucifixion* by Bonino da Campione. From the right of the presbytery one enters the small Xth Cent. *Chapel of St. Linus*. From the left transept, one enters the **Chapel of St. Catherine**, built in 1540, with a large fresco reproducing the *Martyrdom of St. Catherine*, by Lanino (1546).

San Nazaro Maggiore. - Above; detail of the interior of the Trivulzio funeral chapel. Below: the interior of the church.

San Simpliciano. - The façade.

SAN SIMPLICIANO

This is one of the oldest churches in Milan. It was founded by St. Ambrose in the IVth Cent. and constructed, it is believed, upon the site of an ancient pagan cementery. It was then completed by St. Simplicianus who was buried here. The alterations and reconstruction over the centuries, have obliterated the original shape, as the walls of the Early Christian building have been almost completely incorporated into the later structures. Of the façade, which was restored in 1870, only the middle portal is old (XIIth Cent.), the capitals adorned with figures represent the processions of *the Wise Virgins* and *the Foolish Virgins*.

THE INTERIOR, with three aisles still bears visible signs especially on the walls of the nave, of the Early Christian construction. Several paintings of artists of the XVIth and XVIIth Cents. are worthy of note. On the altar of the 3rd chapel of the right aisle, *St. Benedict* by Enea Solmeggia. Beneath the organ pipes, which are in the presbytery, are figures of *Saints* by Aurelio Luini. In the half-vault of the apse, a great fresco executed by Bergognone, around 1515 of the *Coronation of Mary*, a magnificent composition with the Holy Father receiving Jesus and the Madonna in his arms, surrounded by a circle of Angels and Saints.

The Naviglio Canal.

THE NAVIGLIO CANAL

The Canal was built in 1177, when the city was given new walls. This canal, which is fed by the Adda and the Ticino, was intended for irrigation, and to make the various water mills along its banks work; in addition it rechannelled the rivulets and streams flowing in the vicinity of the town, originating the network of canals which exists today: This network centres on the Naviglio Grande, which comes from the Ticino and which was made navigable in 1269 for the transport of marble, for the construction of the cathedral.

After the Naviglio, the *Pavia Canal* was built, to provide water for the park of the Castle of Pavia; next came the picturesque *Martesana Canal* which channelled the waters of the Adda and which led to the building of the Porta Ticinese wharf (Darsena).

Left: **Porta Ticinese (the Gate to the Ticino).** Above: **the Ospedale Maggiore (Great Hospital) called Ca' Granda.**

OSPEDALE MAGGIORE

The Ospedale Maggiore (Greater Hospital), known to the Milanese as *Cà granda* (Greater Hospital) came into being when the thirty or so hospitals in the area of Corso di Porta Romana were housed in a great unified structure. It was founded by Francesco Sforza in 1456 and the first bout lasted until 1497 when Filarete, Solari and Amadeo, worked to build the quadrilateral towards San Nazaro; the second from 1624 when the central part of the façade, the courtyard and the church were built, under the direction of the architects F.M. Richini, G.B. Pessina, F. Mangone and Cerano; the third from 1794 to 1804 when the internal courtyard of the second cross-section and the third side of the façade were built by the engineer P. Castelli. The building was terribly damaged by the 1943 bombings and then reconstructed. It now houses the Rectors' offices, the Faculties of Letters and Law and the governing body of the University.

INDEX